Emerge

EMERGE
Published by EWW
Printed by Amazon Books
United Kingdom

Emerge Worldwide UK, London, United Kingdom CR7 7RU England

All rights reserved. Except for brief excerpts for review purposes, no part of this book may be reproduced or used in any form without written permission from the author.

All scripture quotations, unless otherwise noted, are taken from the Holy Bible, King James Version. Italics in Scripture quotations have been added by the author for emphasis.

www.theemergebook.com

ISBN – 979-8-6270-6449-9

Copyright Emerge Worldwide
The Team: Lynnette Dias, Daniel Reid and Eld Jacqui Heslop
Cover Design: Oliver Greaves
Internal Design: Saint Amoah

Printed in the United Kingdom
First Edition 2020

Emerge

For those who believe there is more

Sharlette E Reid

EWW

For the Reid's,

May this be a year where you emerge completely as the formidable individuals you are. You have always taught me to do the same. May you find deep meaning in the future pathways set before you. May your resolve and unhindered commitment to serving and loving others reach new levels, impacting people from all spheres of life. Go. Be free…live!

For Wendy,

One moment can change a woman's life. One act of obedience can change a generation. May you draw back the curtains with compelling vision and dare to live with no excuses with God. Your love delights and so does your laughter. In all this life, there is something deeply beautiful, may you continue to find it.

And for my Children,

Every child I've taught over the years; may the future never hold your dreams hostile. Go and break all the boxes of limitation. May your ears awaken to your deep callings and may you find Gods pathways for your future.

Contents

Introduction	1-9

THE LAND WITHIN

1. The Knocking	13 - 22
2. The Fast and Focus	23 -39
3. Naked	41-56
4. Core	57-72

THE LAND BEYOND

5. Unexpected Change	75 - 90
6. The Lost Virtue	91-106
7. The Flint, the Diamonds and the Compass	107-128
8. Strangers	129-146

THE ETERNAL LAND

9. Extraction	147-162
10. Critics	163-182
11. Emergency	183-190
12. Emerge	191 -194
Acknowledgements	197
Notes	198-201

Introduction

Reset!

MOMENTS OF deep awakening can happen at any time in our lives, but they are usually provoked by moments of crisis and disruptions. The deep death in the valley has the power to reset our course, and to lead us into the greatest transformations. It can be a time of complete change, a time of radically redefining who we are, and who we are called to be.

Sometimes it is prompted by the deep questions of life such as, 'is this all there is?', 'there must be more to this?', 'what's life's purpose?" and 'where am I going?'.

I found myself asking these questions, not at the beginning of my Christian journey, but somewhere in the middle of it all. Somewhere in life's path I had become enslaved to mediocrity and sameness. I had lost my way in work, social life, my teaching businesses, travelling, ministry and all the highs and lows of life. But, in the early hours of January 2016 it all changed, my life changed. I knew it had to change, I knew I could not continue to live that way.

Introduction

That Morning

Tears washed my face as I lay there.

It was about 2am on a January morning. The world was quiet, but my heart sounded like a relentless beating drum in my chest. I clamoured out of my bed and could do or say little, as I sat in the pitch darkness of my bedroom crying. Between the lonely mumbles, I felt an overwhelming frustration and deep brokenness. Suddenly I shouted above the silence *'I can't do this anymore, there must be more'*. I had no respect for my neighbours, the hour or the other people in my house. I had spent what felt like forever, on the hard floor of my bedroom, in a twisted monologue of past and present issues. I can't even tell you all that I said that night, but I was crushed in Spirit, and I mean crushed! Tears I didn't even know I had, were just flowing like a river whose banks were spilling over and flooding the plains.

I cried to the point where I felt torn and split open, that is the only way I can describe the deep anguish I felt. I moaned with frustration about my life and what I expected at this point, swinging in and out of moments of sorrowful repentance because I knew that somewhere along the path, I had veered off from a unique and authentic relationship with God. I had become numb to the knocking in my spirit and in my soul, that was crying out for more from life. But not that morning, I couldn't escape that morning.

As I lay there like a heap, I could feel the anaesthetic that I had induced myself with over the years, relinquishing its power and hold over me. You know, that 'I'm fine, I'll just smile the day away, keep serving and keep on working' anaesthetic, that so many of us often live off. It keeps you thinking that if you work harder, pushing yourself in order to succeed, that the adrenaline feeling that suppresses the dissatisfaction with the way life is going, will vanish.

Introduction

However, beneath these feelings were hidden anxieties about my future, under the disguise of busyness and activity.

I had convinced myself, that if I just keep on giving, doing and serving, that feeling of unfulfillment will wear off. Well, it hadn't. It hadn't at all.

There was nothing I could tell myself, no verse I could quote, no promise I could recite, no praise I could raise, that could lift me in that morning. There was no prophecy and no smiles of children I had served over the years in missions, that could raise my spirit with hope. I was empty. I was out. I was sobering back up to the deep reality that I wasn't okay. I was far from where I wanted to be in life. I was frustrated, and life had grown deeply mundane and repetitive, all of it! The people, the church services, work, the children I taught and the relationships, they were all one big hum. There was no symphony anymore, there was no deep harmony. My life had become predictable, and over the years I had accepted it! I knew the sound of the drum, and I was happy to dance along to its irregular beat. And slowly, I was drifting across the seas of life and I wasn't even conscious of it.

I had grown accustomed to the unease, anxieties and fears that I held about my future, career, ministry, callings and broader life. There was a comfort in the discomfort, that had become normal. I called that, 'life'. But, that morning the drifter came back to the shore, to realign and gain new direction.

Kneeling down, 'I poured out my heart before the Lord' (Psalms 62:8). It was clear that I needed to reconnect with God at a deeper level. Where I was in my life and relationship with God, had become insufficient, and I had finally accepted and confessed it. I knew God wanted me to be real, I could feel that tug on the inside. I was going to be genuine and frank, and I wasn't going to hold back.

Introduction

Although, I was half tired and exhausted from the crying that morning, I had an inner expectancy as I waited for a new vision, and more information about my future.

I had a rich inner peace which I held onto. However, I also felt like a wife, who had told my husband everything I didn't like about where I was in my life. 'I don't like this, I don't like that, I've messed up here, I've messed up there, I want more of this and that'. I had literally broken down, only to feel like God gracefully walked past me with a loving, peaceful silence the following morning.

You see, there was no radical shift after my breakdown that day. There was no immediate change in that moment, but I did feel open and ready to listen. To be still. I was ready to know whatever God wanted me to know.

In the weeks and months that passed, I continued to pray and seek the Lord. I waited for the bulldoze moment when His presence would manifest strong through a brand new vision, maybe through a dream, prophecy or scripture. I needed direction and I wanted instruction. Instead, throughout that year, God had me reflect on my last 17 years in the faith. I was going through old notepads, reading sermons I wrote years ago, and trawling though prophesies He gave me. The more I read, was the more inadequate and humbled I felt. As I turned the pages of the notepads I had kept over the years, I recognised the fulfilment and faithfulness of Gods promises time and time again.

Over the years, I had learnt so much about serving, humility and trust in God. I had travelled to nations and made grave sacrifices, just based on a word from His Spirit, and oh how I trusted that word. I learnt to love people by simply being there, even for the most vulnerable. I was empowered by the teamwork and submission of colleagues and fellow leaders, who were spreading the gospel from different races and cultures. I had met so many incredible people from politicians, to great international teachers

Introduction

and speakers. I had sat amongst the poor and needy, who taught me my greatest lessons in humility. I had shared the gospel sometimes venturing in rough neighbourhoods, and seen the love and power of God change the hardest of hearts. I had experienced many testimonies of breakthrough, and souls saved in the process. I had even seen His hand of restoration in my own family relationships, as he reconciled my mother and father, something He had showed me years before after they had divorced.

The more I read through my notepads and reflected, was the more I began to give thanks each day to God, with a new found gratitude for all He had already done. I began to praise Him for His grace when I failed, and His unconditional love. He had truly done all He said He would (1 Cor 1:10), protecting, forgiving, keeping me and teaching me.

The more that I sat in awe of Gods hand in my life, was the stronger that my intimacy and desire to seek out the Lord was becoming.

In those months of waiting for God to speak and respond to my cry, I found myself looking back at the times I would sit in the audience ready to preach, hoping that the look on my face and eased smile, would help to conceal the fact that something within didn't feel the same. Something was changing. I hadn't lost my passion to preach or teach, and God was very evidently with me, but I felt a direction change. I, Sharlette Reid had to re-discover myself and God. I needed to know what I was being called away from, and into.

There was so much to learn from the one who 'knit me together' from my mother's womb. I wanted to find that 'special something' again, and I felt that there were deeper depths to be discovered. I knew I would have to let go of some of the information I had held onto, in order to embrace the new knowledge about my identity in

Introduction

God. 'To forget some of the former things', and not to dwell on the past (Isaiah 43:18).

I was ready, ready for the journey, the adventure again. I was ready to live with the full weight of the life merited to me, to discover the new path and surrender to the call.

The journey transformed my life and realigned my perspective. It set me on a new course through open doors of liberty, and freedom of Spirit. Even now, I continue to push beyond all that has concealed me in my life physically, emotionally, spiritually and mentally.

As I emerged, this book was conceived, bringing together the key principles from my own journey. It included the moments before 'that morning', and beyond that moment, until now. It covers the three separate lands: The Land Within, The Land Beyond and The Eternal Land. Each land speaks to the different areas of our life, how we develop personally, how we impact the world around us and how we connect to Gods Eternal Plan for humanity.

The Land Within, was a journey all by itself. I became acquainted with how easily I had fallen into all the trappings of the world, and how I got lost in the busyness and noise. There was a radical need to become conscious of how this was interfering with my ability to hear Gods voice. I was asking for the new, but not able to perceive it.

I was serving and seeing the hand of God move in my life, but until I let go of the vision I was holding onto, I could not receive anything new. I had become closed and I didn't even know it. I had wrapped myself in an old vision and held fast to the roles, positions, activities, and people that surrounded me. I was so busy serving, that I was missing the deep whispers of the spirit. I was hindering my own potential for great change, and in turn living a life of mediocrity.

Introduction

There were many other ills that were affecting my life, such as a lack of intellectual humility, broken areas in need of deep healing, and a need to be open and naked with God. To let Him all the way in.

As I experienced the deep surrender, and submitted to the process of change, I learnt the overarching need to be flexible throughout life's journey. God guided me through the Holy Spirit, with practices that were essential to a healthy spiritual land within. Stillness and rest became my greatest friends, and they both challenged me in ways I could never have imagined, because I was addicted to busyness. Overtime, as I prayed and I learned, I became a land that was open, healed and sensitive to the rhythm and voice of God again. I regained profound peace, gathered real answers and direction in the process.

The Land Beyond, was centred around the need to discern the changes that were happening in my life, as a result of the new callings. As the Holy Spirit completely changed the way I saw myself and the world beyond me, my prayers changed, my outlook changed and my service was delivered with greater obedience to Gods instructions. I discovered parts of Sharlette I had never known and found the joy that comes with salvation again.

I was reminded that my life's vision and calling, was not predicated on a gift or an anointing, neither a title or position. It was simply based on the call and leading of God in any given season. However, I had to sensitise to the signs within, and beyond me, that were leading me along life's course. I had to regain the lost virtue of patience and find the beauty of Gods timing, not running ahead, neither behind.

As I learnt to see the world beyond me, I looked with a new gaze towards the strangers and common people I would usually pass and dismiss, and I had this deep desire to know them. I learnt to

Introduction

see the value of each person I met, to handle them with compassion, love and deep respect.

I felt awake to what was happening around me with new senses and a new level of discernment. I was no longer creating unnecessary tension, and conflict in opposition to the leading in my life, but I was learning the power of deep trust in the unknowns. Adventure and mystery, awe and wonder were rising in me, as I approached each new day with optimism, hope and opportunity. Doors opened up allowing me to use my gifts and talents, new connections and partnerships were formed in my life, and it all seemed to be happening effortlessly. I marvelled at the beauty of living in Gods rhythm, at times it was overwhelming and I just sat and cried.

The Land Eternal, challenged me to completely shift my perspective of the Spirit. I learnt about the Omnipresence of God, and He put to sleep the idea, that everything He wants to do in the earth has to be done through man. God is sovereign, and He wanted to give me a firm reminder of that!

I learnt great humility as I began to see my footprint in life, as no greater or significant than anyone-else's. I learnt that I was joining an Eternal movement that began way before I entered the world: *'to seek and to save'* lost humanity. And it was amazing, because I never saw it as a movement, that revelation alone, transformed my whole mind. There was a need to remain Eternally Conscious of a life beyond this three dimensional one, as a way of not getting lost again in the attractiveness, and busyness of the world beyond.

I now live with such value again in human life, as I have learnt to commit to greater service, and to share the gospel more intentionally. I am living in pleasant peace, with deeper meaning and commitment to my new path. I handle life more loosely and

Introduction

I've let go of the false sense of control. Now I can bask in times of surreal refreshing.

However, I am convinced and convicted, that we are all called to Emerge, and that is why this book is not just about me, it's also about you. This book details my own experiences, with anecdotes to support you in your own journey. There are practical questions, to help you discover where you are in life, and not where you imagine you are. There are plenty of lessons to help you as you identify what has concealed, hidden and prevented you from living the way God intended.

Whether you believe in the afterlife or not, you get an opportunity now to leave footprints in the sand of the places you go, and handprints in the hearts of those you transform in the world. But, that gift and value in life, is awakened when you live in Gods purpose, and understand your callings pushing forward with a commitment to change.

It's time to move beyond where you are, and to become sensitive to Gods leading. As you learn to listen again, and to come into the truth concerning Gods plans for your life, may you enter out of the darkness of thought, experience, spirit, knowledge and pride. Step into the glorious light of wholeness, healing and purpose. It's time for you to connect to Gods rhythm, and play a greater part in the Eternal Movement.

People are waiting to receive you.
It's time to **Emerge.**

The Land Within

CHAPTER ONE

The Knocking

There was darkness in a way that none of you will ever experience. The gushing waters moved with a gentle toing, and froing, inwards and then out. The earth sat like a quiet deserted land in a state of emptiness, as the Spirit hovered over the waters. Suddenly, there was a sound that brought in a rupturing of the old state, and the creation of the new. The earth listened in the dark quietness, to Gods voice, and responded by taking on a whole new form. That sound was an invitation for new life, and the emerging of a new day.

CAN YOU hear the sound on the inside? It's that knocking telling you that there's more?

At times the knocking can arise through a bold invitation in your life, like an envelope that drops though your letterbox unexpectedly. It could be a sudden disruption, a shift in your health, finance, life's path or a sudden diagnosis, that causes you to sit up and take note, to ask or search for deeper meaning, and a greater calling. For others, it can arise more subtly, through a gentle inner tug, and a gut wrenching pulling in your spirit, that seems to surface in different moments of your life. No matter what you do, you can't seem to shake it. Some of you may be experiencing that feeling now!

No matter where and who you are, saved and unsaved, you need to grab hold of this truth. You were designed, created and made, for more than the life you are currently living, and this journey is there to awaken you to that again! To discover it, to search for it, and to live it!

> *'I believe that we all encounter the knock at the door of our lives, most rarely hear it amidst the noise of life, those who do, often ignore it, but a few choose to answer'.*

Even as I look back on my own journey, I wonder how long the deep knocking had been taking place in my life, was it days, weeks, months or even years? I had become so engrossed, and distracted by my daily activities of working, serving, socialising, travelling and teaching, that somewhere along the line, I was no longer 'fully' depending on the leading of the Spirit. I got caught up in a wild fury of activities, stressful and pressing deadlines, personal goals, and regular social interactions. And yet it was clear, that amongst what I was calling life and Godly service, was dysfunction, and it had caught up with me once and for all. It was only a matter of time, before some level of mental, emotional, spiritual or physical breakdown would have hit my life.

When I broke down in floods of tears, in the early hours of that January morning in 2016, crying out with desperation that there must be more, it was just the tipping point. I had been fighting with inner tensions, and drowning out the noise of mediocrity and boredom, for years. Even though I felt this way, I wasn't telling God, I wasn't expressing it. The more that I ignored it, was the more I became numb to the feeling.

What I was missing, was that the knocking was an invitation for more. It was being quietly whispered on the inside of me, whilst I was trying to muzzle it for years. Although I could hear God, I simply wasn't responding in this area, and the deep feeling of discontentment with life, continued to grow. My commitment grew relentlessly, in all the areas I was serving and working. Busyness kept me occupied.

However, it was through my emergence that I learned again, that you can't enter into meaningful relationship with the Spirit of God, and be run rugged with the same, if not more, activities and noise of the world. Aside from the mental and physical exhaustion, it will become painfully hard to listen to God. This in turn will affect how you navigate through life.

As I went through my process of change, and engaged with many men and women at work, at church, and in social gatherings, it became deeply apparent to me that so many others had lost their sensitivity to Gods voice. Some mentioned that despite services, prayer meetings, work and great salaries, home life, social life and friends, there was some deep unrest! A disconnect. There was a frustration with life and discomfort. The coping strategy was to become more subdued in activities, and busyness. The harder the feeling, knocking and tug came, to get their attention, was the more they turned up the noise of life, so they could drown it out! They engaged in more social activities, spent more time on their phones, messages, and registered for more conferences. That way they were less inclined to hear it, and hopefully no-one else would either!

Unfortunately, I believe this is how many people are choosing to live. Maybe, even you! But, it's time to lean in and listen, to be open and to respond to the knocking.

Lean in and listen

One of the greatest challenges of our age is to listen. With so much noise all around, so many people have become deafened to Gods voice.

The reality is that in our modern culture, some of you can't function without noise. Whether it's the noise of music, the phone calls and messages, or modernisation and development, the world is noisy. This constant festival of noise in the atmosphere and environments of the mind, are bombarded by constant negative news from media outlets, creating an unhealthy state of fear and anxiety. And the cherry on the cake, is the noise of others expectations and opinions, about the way you should live your life. Noise is everywhere and the demands that increased connectivity places on you, add to that.

This generation has become so noisy, that the World Health Organisation said that: 'Silence is a precious commodity that is disappearing', after tracking it for the last decade (W.H. O 2020). Also, in its *Guidelines for Community Noise*, the W.H.O declared, "Worldwide, noise-induced hearing impairment is the most prevalent irreversible hazard, and it is estimated that 120 million people worldwide have been affected." It's a staggering number, but it is indicative of modern culture. Who would've thought that noise would become one of the greatest challenges, in cultivating a healthy spiritual life!

In the 21st Century' it's as if we have all grown accustomed to noise, and the constant demand for engagement. Noise has even permeated the churches, with many people searching for times of peace and sanctum. Just a moment's stillness amongst the worship, to allow people to listen and discern Gods presence, can be hard to find.

At times, I have felt that the older Church allowed more time for sacred silence, to be still, to reverence and to hear the voice of God speak clearly, right there in the moment of the service. They encouraged the need to let the spirit lead. A practice and discipline that, some may argue, wouldn't go amiss in the modern church. Do 'the weary and burdened find rest' in the church anymore? are they learning how to discern God's presence in the stillness? (Matt 11:28) or has it become congested with more activities and a constant need for noise? Either way, the onus is not on an institution, the world or anyone else to lead you back to a place of listening again. No, you must walk that path for yourself with God.

Your most important work begins here.

'Creating a lifestyle of listening must be done intentionally, or it will be near to impossible to hear what you need to, as you emerge in this journey'

Be honest

The first thing that some of you need to be open to, is the beauty of vulnerability and honesty.
Let's be true with one-another throughout this journey, and real with God.

Some of you have been going through the motions, the activities, the attendance, and fulfilling the demands of life. You may even be giving of your time, attending meetings, engaged in social impact and trying to be a good role model for those around. But, the passion, the intentional commitment and joy of serving God has dissipated for some of you. If you're honest, some of you feel stuck in a rut, in a role, organisation or position in life, even though you are no longer growing or thriving anymore, and you know it!

The good news is, that no matter what has blocked the way or concealed you in life, it's never too late to flourish in the path and callings God has for you. The truth may be, that you've grown so attached to your current calling, roles and responsibilities that the thought of stepping away is terrifying, especially if you are a leader. On the other hand, you may have lost the necessity to know God. Your routines, successes, sense of achievement, appetites whether good or bad, and interests, may be calling you in a different direction. Some of those interests, may be driven by Spiritual strongholds directing your life, which are pulling you away from the leading of the Spirit. At times, there are deeper reasons for this as you will explore in this book, but let's consider further, how critical your response is now.

The famous scripture in Psalms 23:5 says:

> *'He has prepared a table for you in the*
> *presence of your enemies'*

It's a classic example of how God gives you opportunities to positively grow. To recognise where you are, and to perceive that right before you, there is more. This conscious awareness, is not about anyone else's life except for your own. You have to see what's in the room you stand in, clearly. That room is your life.

I want you to imagine your favourite meal with the finest cutlery laid out. That meal represents new callings, positions, places or people. But that sumptuous, delicious, and delightful meal, will lay sitting there, year after year. It's not moving anywhere, no-ones coming to steal it, time can't hinder it, but you have to perceive it through the Spirit, to listen and move towards it. You may not be able to see what's on the table, and you may even struggle initially to hear anything new, but don't be afraid to cry out as I did that morning, and wait for the answer (Jer 33:3) The answer is there.

It's time to emerge from the noise, the counter rhythm, and collective patterns of the world. Don't limit your potential, and stagnate your purpose.

The word Emerge, means: to *'appear by coming out of something or out from behind something'* (Cambridge Dictionary). To no longer ignore, be intimidated, concealed or hidden behind a world, a system, or any other spirit, that is hindering your growth and renewal.

As you push forward and take the seat, as you invite the new into your life though prayer. You are going to see your enemies, and you'll have to make a choice. You will either confront them or not. Not my enemies, yours. The enemies within you, and the enemies beyond you.

I too had to do this, to take a seat at the table and face the enemies to my life's purpose head on, because it was an essential part of the journey. No-one forced me to, I wanted to. I believed that 'He that lives in me, is truly greater than anything in the world', or any inner voice or fears I had. I trusted the knocking. I trusted Gods voice! And what made the journey so powerful, was that He never left me to sit and eat alone, in the presence of my enemies instead 'He sat and dined with me' (Rev 3:20)

In the same way, I pray that you too, will choose to venture forward, to discover the path set before you, because it's beautiful!

> *'You already know what you know, you've travelled the same journey again and again each day in your life, it's predictable. You know it's not enough and that ought to push you beyond. God is calling you to where you haven't been, to seek out what you don't know about your life, God and the future'.*

Open your eyes

As you surrender to listening and find new form in the journey, I pray that you can also awaken to the new vision, and where it calls you.

You are not going to be given a picture of a future that you can establish on your own, but a vision that causes you to depend on Gods 'all sufficiency to get you there'. That vision may arrive in many ways through the: small still voice, the word, through dreams, scriptures or visions. He may ask you to pack up and leave for a new country like Abraham, or to help build a neighbouring area like Nehemiah. Whether you take a stand against injustice like Moses, preach in persecuted lands like Paul or govern nations like Joseph; most of the visions God gives, go beyond your realised perceptions of self and future. No matter what you have experienced before, prepare for the extraordinary!

> *'The most beautiful thing you can experience is the mysterious. He to whom this emotion is stranger, who can no longer*

The Knocking

pause to wonder and stand rapt in awe, is as good as dead: his eyes are closed.'

Albert Einstein

Even in my own journey, I began to recognise that somewhere in our humanity to try and understand God, we have lost the real awe and sovereignty of who He is. We have forgotten He exists in bountiful power and brilliance, whether we exist or not. That in our greatest effort to humanise God, so that we may understand Him, many have begun to form God in their own image. Some are guilty of stripping away some of His glorious attributes such as holiness, the only truth, the only way, as they try and make God fashionable, and relatable for a new generation.

All of these things create barriers, that make it incredibly hard to reverence and believe, that someone 'who is like you; can offer you a life that is greater! Too often, this opens the door for human pride or logic, to refute a greater vision for your life.

Have you become inflexible and limited by your own perspective of who God is? Could this be causing an apathy and resistance to change? Don't let that destroy your chance to live out abundance, to flourish, to at least give your life an opportunity to live beyond the borders of your own vision of the future.

As you accept the invitation through real confession and deep prayer to God, may you emerge with new life and power.

New roads lie ahead for you, as you sensitise again to the knocking in your life. It's time to listen, and to live with new and un-borrowed vision. I pray that this journey encourages you to *'press forward towards the prize of the 'higher calling, in Christ Jesus'* (Phil 4:3), despite the current comforts and busy culture of our time.

As the journey begins on a personal level, make some steps towards listening:

- Create times of stillness, deep reflection and open, honest prayer throughout this transformative journey
- Ask God to re-connect your listening to the rhythm of the Holy Spirit
- Ask for His Divine help, as you begin to see yourself and your life, the way He does
- Finally, ask Him to reawaken your sense of adventure and ability to perceive the new

CHAPTER TWO

Fast and focus!

Rest and focus, are both key to recognising the direction of your life. But sometimes, you have to go to great lengths to find it.

I KNOW that the competing interruptions from life and people, can make it hard to discern or focus on anything in this age. I'm familiar with the demands from home, work, study, children, church, the cat, and the dog, all vying for your attention! Everything is constantly shouting 'me, me, look here, be there, with the barrage of messages, notifications, and WhatsApp's'. At times, it's enough to make anyone scream, and maybe some of you have! 'I just need a break, a moment and a hush', you may feel.

Well, I've been there!

There were seasons of my life when I would tell my friends that I was in 'the cave'. My cave still exists, when I critically need stillness and escape. It's not a place in the outback of Australia, neither in the mountains of some Tibetan landscape, it's in my extension, the attic of my home. I would close the door, switch off my phone, and just lie on the floor. Sometimes, I would fill the atmosphere with instrumentals of worship and at other times I would listen to the sounds of nature on YouTube, like the rushing waters or the sound of the wind. As long as I was in my cave, I didn't want to be bothered. I needed time on my own, and I needed to stop the constant noise and hum of the world, because it was becoming unbearable at times. And for some of you reading this, you may have learned to cope in the same way. You might find yourself shutting off from the world and those close to you, just to find some respite and re-focus again, snatching a moment here and a moment there.

You see, during my emergence I couldn't tell you the last time I had travelled to the attic. I had lost the still quiet moments, and at times I was struggling to get off of the Ferris wheel of activity, that I was on. Instead I was waking daily after times of prayer and ready to rock on with a new day, in for the highs and for the lows, crashing out at the end of it all. There was no snatching of time here and there, I was getting rest when I slept. My body was used to being on the go, and my life was seriously overcrowded with activities. I was so busy, that I only looked forward to rest, when I was booking my next holiday!

Growing up, I was never really taught to see rest as an important spiritual discipline. So, this was a serious lesson for me, and one of the biggest!

Rest is an important time for regeneration, the way your body lives, thrives and survives, using the information it receives and creates...Rest should be seen as: physical rest, mental rest, social rest and spiritual rest. (Matt.J. Edlund M.D)

It's time to, *'come away by yourselves to a secluded place, and rest a while'* (Mark 6:31, Luke 4:42)

Let's be honest, most of you rarely have time for you. Somewhere along the course of life, you may have learned that a quiet moment, where nobody is talking, and the television or phone is off, is a bad thing. You are missing out! A moment's rest becomes a mind-conference of stressful planning, strategies, and lists. It's like a tennis court of constant thoughts, back and forth. In those moments, you can feel guilty that you are making time for yourself. Just as you sit and rest, you hear this voice telling you: 'there's plenty that you could be getting done with the time, instead of sitting or lying here'. 'Look at the clothes, you've haven't cooked yet and you don't have time for this!'. The inner voice usually sounds like your most annoying school teacher! And just like that, you're up finding something else to do.

If that's you, you're not alone, there's a whole bunch of us who are still learning how to still the rushing in our minds, and take time for ourselves.

Mind UK, an organisation that supports those with mental health problems, said:

> *'In our hectic lives, we sometimes forget to check in with ourselves. Therefore, we sometimes don't realise our wellbeing is suffering until we are struggling because of it'. (Mind 2013)*

At times, I believe that it's easy to neglect your self-care, because few people in your life will ask you, if you've been resting, have you had a break? or have you stopped? Furthermore, not everyone cares for your wellbeing as much as they care for your well doing. They are far too consumed in your outputs, results, and visible activities. They want you at that party smiling and looking happy, in that conference room delivering your perspectives, at their services serving, to respond to their calls, and to work in their jobs and tasks. But how well are you taking care of your physical, spiritual, emotional, and psychological health?

If you neglect this area of your life, it will cause you to miss an essential time to heal and recharge. This may even be a reason why so many of you are not perceiving the knocking in your life. You are exhausted, tired, and fatigued. You are caught up in an unhealthy routine. Dragging yourself out of bed each day, to do the rat race all over again, without any time for real rest in God's presence, will begin to affect your life negatively. You have to run from the rush of life, the mad pursuit and the chaos of it all, if not, you will damage your health through stress and breakdowns. And your tender mind will be devoid of renewal as you become a slave to every urgent thought and distracting activity.

It's time to get rid of the clutter

The more cluttered and loud your mind becomes, the harder it is to perceive the presence of God in your life. If you are like me, you're going to have to look at how you are managing your time and activities better. You can no longer live your lives to the beat of an irregular drum. I mean, no-one's going to give you a special bow or badge, for the number of activities you were engaged in when you reach the end of your life. 'Why not?', you may ask. Because living is not about busyness and the amount of activity you are engaged in. Neither is motion a sign of progress or development.

It's time to stop living like passengers on a flight called busyness, towards a destination called nowhere.

As some of you read this, it's a good time to ask yourself, 'are the activities I am engaged in actually lining up with my sense of calling, or am I throwing my time, energy and focus everywhere and nowhere?'.

It's easy to be fuelled by being on the constant go, but where's it all going? I say this because I have been there. I have loved so many things. I have wanted to do as much as I can with the life I've been given. I would be thinking of ways to help on the mission field, to empower an emerging generation, to teach and reach more people with the gospel of Jesus Christ. How can I get more people into employment? How can I mentor all these people? I was at the networking events, the conferences, and the training, but it was energy and activity spread wide and thin. I wasn't focused. This led to me spending minimal time on my own passions, projects, and people, because I felt compelled to support here, there, and everywhere. But, I was only doing myself and others a disservice, because I was too exhausted to focus my time and energy in the areas I was actually called to. Hence, my word of caution to you, is that there is nothing wrong with you wanting to accomplish so much or having so many plans, ideas, and passions, but you must prioritise and focus it in the area 'you are being called'. Separating what you want to do, versus what you need to do, in any given season of your life is essential.

It's time to find rest and focus again, and to be sensitive to the voice within.

Re-gaining focus

I remember a conversation with my mother around focus. I knew that I had received clear instructions through dreams and prayer, to focus on developing projects in particular areas. However, I was inconsistent. One minute I'd be praying strong, focused and committed to listening and building the projects I needed to, researching and excited. The next minute, the same zeal, passion and commitment, would dwindle and fade as I grew distracted. It was a constant cycle of up's and downs! I wouldn't even feel the shift. Whilst speaking to my mother about it, I arrived at some answers. The first, was that my routine needed to change, from the moment I rolled out of bed to the moment I fell asleep. My old routine just wasn't working. The inconsistency was delaying and hindering my personal productivity and progress. I knew I HAD to make some changes!

I remember sitting in my garden not so long after the conversation. I had decided to alter my routine, and to sit for an hour each morning on my own. I left my phone, embraced the day and took my big, grey fluffy blanket, to sit on the dark green chair on the patio, facing the morning sun. The first two days, felt like a struggle because my mind wanted to be entertained by my usual stimulus of phones calls and the morning emails. Besides, I had fed my mind a diet of sensory overload - a little focus on the computer, on the phone, at work, reading notifications, thinking about tomorrow, worrying about today and multi-tasking. And that was the problem.

Caroline Beaton wrote in Forbes (2017) that 'multitasking', which was first formed as a word for computers not humans, in a 1964 IBM paper, is changing our brains. The problems were listed as 'compromising our visual awareness, dividing attention, distracting and sabotaging our overall performance'.

It was clear that the side effects were already manifesting in my life. They may even be manifesting in yours! However, I was intentional to escape the urge of dispensing my attention everywhere, and to re-learn focus one task at a time.

I wanted to find the value of silence again, so I committed to seeking out the reprieve that nature had to offer by sitting outside.

In that time, I actually realised how much I took the natural world around me for granted. My senses were so assailed to city life, the bustling sound of traffic, people rushing by with their phones going off, cars speeding by and mixed voices. I'd get home with a headache, a nose full of fumes, tired and exhausted, and get ready to do it all again the day after. Is there any wonder disconnect had crept in!

Some mornings I watched the birds, hearing their song, looking at the slow dance of the leaves on the trees, and feeling the wind against my skin. I watched as the gentle winds of change graced the skies, causing the trees to rock with direction east and west, fully surrendered to the movement beyond, and I marvelled at its submission.

I would reflect on the simplicity and value of life, just life with nothing added. My gratitude to see a new day, my empty moments to listen and quietness to pray, stilled my mind and soul. I never consciously took the time to enjoy the nature and life around me. To allow Gods ministry of creation to speak to my anxious heart, and yet in those moments I found such a delicate peace.

Could your life be in need of a rich indulgence in nature? Maybe a gentle walk in the park, looking outside in a well-kept garden, sitting by the lake, or retreating to the forest, could all offer some well needed rest.

Science has proven, through several studies on participants who went for nature walks in Japan and Finland, that: *'being in nature has a profound impact on our brains, and our behaviour, helping us to reduce anxiety, brooding, and stress, and increase our attention capacity and creativity'*. (Greater Good Magazine 2016)

Within the first week of adopting this practice in my own life, I realised that my whole spirit, mind and work changed. It was clear that my mind had been in desperate need for the hour away each morning. I had time to be still and I felt clear about the key activities of the day. I wrote lists each morning and became much more intentional about how I spent my time. After some time in silence, listening, I would read scripture and begin to offer my mornings prayers. As I did, I felt a sense of enhanced sensitivity to Gods voice and recorded the information in my journal as I heard it. I refined the information that I was allowing to pass through me, by limiting the mornings distractions. This diffused a lot of unnecessary thinking and stress before the day had even started. I had always taken time to pray and be still, but it wasn't like this.

I remain committed to this action each day, though some mornings, outside wasn't the best place to sit, so I would reposition myself, and find a new space in my bedroom! It was all part of my personal adjustment. Rest was becoming my friend. It was no longer an enemy to purpose denying me of time, but gifting me with the withdrawal that I needed from the cares of the world. The offer of safe space in God's presence, was right there.

I wonder what you may find in your times of quiet? I wonder what could be waiting for you in your rest, that you can't perceive as long as you are committed to a world of noise? Don't just hear my account, this is in the Bible! Although you don't often hear most teachers speaking on the power of rest, except in wellbeing seminars and workshops, it is there in the word.

Jacob, a man in Genesis 28:10 - 16, left his home to journey to Mesopotamia. Jacob was tired and exhausted. Mentally, emotionally and physically, that he couldn't go further without resting in the journey. He stayed in an unusual place, between two lands and grabbed some stones to lie on. He stopped and waited there all night, *'because the sun was set'*.

What a beautiful picture! Can you imagine Jacob being still and admiring nature, as the beautiful mid oranges, reds and yellows in the sky, arrayed their beauty? He lay down in that place and fell asleep. Whilst sleeping he had an extraordinary vision and dream about his future, his children and the land he was coming into. (verse 13-15) He awoke from the dream and marvelled, *'surely the Lord was in this place and I knew it not'*. Wise words from a tired man.

I find it remarkable that as Jacob stopped and got still, he found that God was right there in that place of quiet. I imagine he was shocked to know that a moment's rest could bring such revelation. God was masterfully waiting for Jacob in the quiet, with answers and revelation about his future, and Jacob wasn't even looking for it. It wasn't in the noise, the dance, the shout, the prayer, but actually as he rested!

> *Oh, how you can underestimate the power*
> *of a rested mind, in order to perceive what*
> *the spirit of God is saying*

Although rest and stillness is a necessity for some of you, and it sounds easy, it's a major feat! The mind forms habits and practices that are hard to break. Some of you have had months and years of overcrowding in your mind. Thoughts are running everywhere like a supermarket where the children are out of hand running from aisle to aisle. You're constantly anxious due to the bombardment and impact of those thoughts, and your spirit and mind need a drastic re-alignment. You're going to need more than birds and trees in the morning, a sunset or a still moment. Yes! It's time to acquaint yourself with the power that fasting can bring!

Fasting – Quiets the Soul bringing depth and intimacy

> *'You must be prepared to gift your future with extraordinary levels of discipline, spiritual alignment and commitment'.*

Some of you have been putting off fasting, but I'm calling you out!

Quieting the soul where our emotions and feelings run wild, and awakening to the whispers of the spirit, is unlocked powerfully though fasting. There are some answers that arrive only through fasting and prayer. (Matt 17:21)

Fasting is defined as the ability *'to eat no food for a period of time' (Cambridge dictionary.* It is not a mysterious and mystical concept. Even, if you look up 'fasting' today, you get a mountain of videos, articles, podcasts and research on new findings based on the explosion of interest. People want to know more about what happens to our bodies and spirits, when we fast. But, I'm not just speaking about passing up the plate, or using it as a vehicle to lose weight. The biblical principle of fasting has been seen as a way to break you out of the world's routine, and sensitise you to Gods leading in your life, bringing incredible spiritual breakthroughs. It can loose chains, and break strongholds that have been wrecking your life and keeping you in cycles.

The aim is to feed yourself with God's word, times of prayer, stillness and worship. To do this effectively, you will need to pull away from some of the non-essential activities and people, because focus will require you to wean yourself from distractions.

During my time of fasting from food, I enjoyed limited times of communication. I refused to answer calls or be on social media, and I made people aware. This was part of me disconnecting from the noise culture. It also helped me to create long uninterrupted moments of focused time, whilst studying the word and praying.

Fasting doesn't grant you immunity from others who may want to defray your attention in any given season, however, it does give you the inner strength to push past physical and spiritual resistance, as you open up to the Holy Spirit and listen. The power of fasting helps you to radically shift your focus, and sensitises you to spirits, thoughts and behaviours, that may be stifling your surrender to Gods path.

The first thing you need to do, is to be clear about the specific purpose of your fast. Are you seeking God's guidance? (Judges 20:26) humbling yourselves before him? (Psalms 35:13) Are you requiring clarity with the work and tasks he has for you? (Nehemiah 1:3) or overcoming temptations and dedicating yourself to him? (Matt 4:1-11) Whatever it is, be clear.

Depth

By stilling your mind and focusing on the leading of the Holy Spirit of God throughout your fast, you will be increasing your depth of intimacy with the creator. The Holy Spirit is sent to 'teach us all things' (John 14:26) and direct us throughout this course of life, and that learning 'never' stops. The spirit doesn't just live beyond you, but inside of you (2 Kings 4:7). You have access to the vast intelligence, knowledge, heart and breadth of all there is to know about life and godliness. So, I encourage you to come into your fast ready to be liberated. As you receive new knowledge and revelation, it will change what you see, how you pray and how you behave, so be open.

There's no one size fits all approach when entering into God's presence. In different seasons the way you enter in your times of prayer can change.

I was always taught to *'enter with thanksgiving and praise'*, when it came to prayer (Psalms 100:4). The mothers in the church where I grew up, used to say that, and so I would always begin with a heart of gratitude ready to spill over with thanks. However, during my emergence, the Lord had me sitting in silence, and even stopped me as I was about to sing. It was that moment of 'not today Sharlette, thank you very much', hand in face feeling! I was taken back, was I hearing correctly? I was, but God wanted to teach me a new way, He wanted me to be still, and to reverence Him as God. He didn't want me running ruggedly into His presence, ready to lumber Him with my thoughts and plights of the day. It was bizarre, but I knew what I heard.

As I came into prayer, I began in silence, I wanted to talk and at times I did, then I'd fall back into a silence. It was funny at times, because I realised how much I love to talk when it comes to prayer. It was such a new practice, but I was open to learning. I waited on God each day. That time helped me to be fully in the moment, to be calm and ready to engage in prayer, and listening.

My Fast and focus

I will never forget a particular 'defining fast', as I journeyed through my emergence. The fast was incredibly revealing and extremely focused. At the time, I heard a quiet inner voice beckoning me to do an extended fast, for a month- 3am -3pm daily.

I began the fast shortly after a relationship breakup. It was hard, because this one was the closest to marriage.

We had already gone looking at rings, planning wedding locations, and I had already thought out all the plans and changes that would need to happen before our lives were bound together. However, it was not God's plan that we stayed together. After a year, we were already caught in disagreements and taking very different paths. It had all come together very quickly, but it fell apart just as fast.

It was a door that God closed, and it was essential as part of the transition, because you:

> *'can't take people along a path in life they're not meant to tread. You have to find peace as each person takes their own course'.*

I knew that I had made the right decision to end the relationship, and I also felt the inner tug, that I had to do this fast. So I prayed, and I felt God challenge me to do a month. What?! I initially felt. I must've heard wrong. So I prayed more than once, and the answer never changed. I can't stand when that happens! I made up in my mind that I was committed to unlearning and re-learning whatever I must, to move forward with my life. All I knew was that I refused to come out of the fast, without some answers, and a deeper level of healing. I was ready to lean in and listen.

During my fast, I was up early, though I struggled hard at the start. I was also glad that I ended at 3pm before I headed to my schools to teach my children, or they would've had the Grinch for a teacher. During the course of my fast, I began being totally transparent about my failings and poured out my heart concerning my regrets and personal shame. I felt so personally embarrassed by so many of my decisions, oftentimes wondering how did I get there? I also realised there were areas where I had become so hardened in my heart and resistant to really accepting the need to change, especially in my character. The resistance was real! I could often get easily impatient, frustrated and stubborn. These weaknesses were highlighted to me during my fast, as areas I drastically needed to change.

My will was breaking, especially during the middle of a thirty days fast where I barely missed food, and would drink bottles of water until I was peeing it regularly. (Sorry! A bit unladylike, but I just want to be real with you).

There was a lot of prayer, a lot of tears and plenty of quietness. Some of the quietness was because I didn't have as much physical energy as usual to talk, so I tried to speak only as I felt led. Through less talking, I learnt to slow down, and really think about what I was saying from day to day

I felt re-energised and invigorated by the Holy Spirit, although some mornings my physical energy was low. I kept unnecessary activities and social commitments to a minimum. No to weekends out, too many drives, restaurant eats or too much noise. My hearing was clear, and I wanted to keep it that way.

A deep inner unity between me and God, was building in the quiet exchanges of the spirit. At times I felt compelled to raise a sound of praise. I would start singing songs, that the church mothers used to sing when I first became a Christian, like 'Rock of Ages', 'Spirit of the living God, fall a fresh on me'. All I needed was a few layers of clothes, kitten heels and a broach, and I could've passed for one of the church mothers.

The more that I read and studied the bible, was the more that the Lord reinforced new beliefs around my health, family, finance, thinking, relationships and soul winning. As He equipped me through His word, this became the main source of my communication. The word was changing and correcting me daily (Heb 4:12). The Spirit in me was awakening with strength, joy and excitement.

What amazed me further, were the powerful visions I had over that time and the dreams. I saw myself doing things I never thought I could whilst travelling to India, America more frequently, and even Africa. This was not visualisation or some meditative technique, it was the powerful Spirit of God revealing the future to me. They all made sense like a jigsaw puzzle, finally coming together. Pieces of the future course were taking shape.

Part of the revelation I received, was around a greater work that I had to complete with a new charity. It was a bit sketchy at the time, but I knew it had to do with healing.

Some nights, names of women I didn't know, were placed in my spirit to pray for. I would begin praying and then hear a name mentioned loudly in my spirit. There were nights I prayed until I wept for women I've never met. Somewhere deep within, I was bonding to the assignment of the Lord, and the burden for women was becoming evident and real.

I began to adjust my routine, with a balanced prayer lifestyle, and solid time to start the new projects that I felt God was calling me to. I used the time to prioritise my goals and activities.

After completing the month, I was different. My friends said I had changed, and my best friend said, 'I feel like I'm getting to know you from the beginning'. She was telling no lies! I felt different after 30 days. My spirit was strong and I felt realigned with a new path. I was looking at everything differently.

My first stop, after I returned from a ministry trip to New York was to meet with my spiritual father. We met for lunch, in a lovely small Greek restaurant, the food was lovely. During our catch up, he stopped and mentioned his surprise, that I had survived a break-up from some-one I thought I would marry, and yet be so positively enthused with life, so forgiving, so soon. 'I can't even smell the smoke on you' he said.

What he didn't know, was that I cried a lot during that fast, but I was also very honest and I knew I made the right choice to step away. The work wasn't complete, but the fast helped to initiate the healing that ensued over that year, and the residue attached to it.

I knew that my spirit had been crying out for renewal, I just had to be still enough, to receive what I needed in God's presence. Though I had fasted before, this was something quite memorable and distinctively life altering. God was pouring out like a wellspring, so much detail about the next steps of my life. There was expediency to the flow of information, and also the process of inner healing.

God is ready to direct you along the new course and path, but how far will you go to hear Him. You can't afford to miss these times of renewal because you're stuck in a counter rhythm, and an old routine!

Change is here!

Some of you are in desperate need for spiritual hydration and replenishment, through fasting. To put your flesh and your body in a position that deprives its dependency on physical strength, and to water your spirit.

It's time to surrender your life to closer examination. The personal cost of staying where you are without inner growth, is more than any external gain the world can offer.

What's been holding you back? What's lingering in the coves of your life?

Everything may tell you that 'you can't do it', 'it's long', but you can and you will. It will take will power, but you will find great truth in His presence. You will also restore focus and depth in your intimacy with God. Take the journey into liberty through His presence. Do what it takes to understand your calling in this season, to make the right choices and adjust your routine where necessary.

You may need some time away from the kids, work, the husband, wife or friends. It may even require you to step away from some commitments and social circles, as you tilt towards focus again. But, if you are to open your spirit to listening again, you have to intentionally regain your focus in a fast world, and starve your distractions.

Whatever the cost, it will be worth it.

Sometimes God's just waiting for you!

CHAPTER THREE

Naked - the dressing room

'As long as your roots are still stuck in the soil of your past, it will be impossible for you to move forward'

WE ALL need a dressing room. I'm not speaking of the place where you cut your beards, put on make-up and change your clothes – because most of you will have a space like that in your homes. However, I'm speaking of the type of dressing room that allows you the private space to retreat away; a space where you can look deep into the waters of your own reflection. This space allows time for you to discover, who you are and where you are, in life. It's necessary to steal this time away, because the busyness of life can keep you blinded from your actual position, and from recognising some of the barriers to your growth. This will cause you to remain stifled because:

Naked

> *'In order for you to change, you must first understand where you actually are'*

You may be loved for the person you project: anointed, ambitious, accomplishing, gaining, respected and wealthy, but none of these are signs that you are whole within. In fact, some of you may be conscious that you are living with deep fractures in the clay of your life, that seep out every now and again. Some of you have done your best to patch up the broken pieces, in order to keep on going. Not surprisingly, the wounds will eventually seep out into your life.

Neglect in this area will always prevent you from making deep inner change, which results in you being held back by old ways and habits. I've known people to succeed in life, marriage, business and ministry, and then to endure public or private humiliation, personal breakdowns and deep physical, emotional and mental loses. They could only watch on painfully as their private wounds were publicly displayed. This is why the dressing room is one of the most important areas in your life, it's where deeper emotional and spiritual healing can take place. Where your wounds can be attended to.

I can confess that the dressing room is not a celebrated place, and not even a place that's remarked about. But in the words of actor, producer and photographer, Michael Kushner:

> *'what happens on the stage of life demonstrates brilliance. What happens beforehand demonstrates... dedication'*

Michael Kushner (2017)

It's incredibly true. No one goes to a West End theatre and starts talking about the dressing room. They are busy praising the execution and craft of acting, the staging and magnificent lighting, the whole production of it all. But the dressing room is where the real change takes place, as these ordinary people who have spent hours, days, weeks and months studying their character and morphing into new roles, now stand ready to serve the audience a winning performance.

The truth is, few people genuinely care much for what happens with you and to you, beyond the moments they share with you. Most people in your life indulge in your daily performance, with no real appreciation for the dedication, endurance and surrender it takes, to keep on going, keep on giving and keep on doing! Can I get an amen!! They have no idea of your internal struggles, brokenness, the stresses, anxieties or strains that you have to overcome. They don't notice the inner war beneath the smiles, and the same daily routines; and for some, you pray they never will. However, there are times in life when you need to strip down, and lay your life out bare. But this isn't easy, definitely not in our current culture of perfection. Many people find it hard to be vulnerable, in any way shape or form.

Have you become a victim of the great cover-up?

The Cover-up

The greatest cover-up of our generation, is behind the filter, the masks and the barrage of images. The crisis is glamourous, identities are strangled, and the death is silent

Pretty strong you may say, but deeply true. There are never-ending flawless and photo-shopped images of perfect men, and women on all types of advertising. From television, billboards, social media to magazine covers. People go to great lengths to cover their flaws. How do you think the plastic surgery market has become a multi-million-pound industry? From body contouring, butt implants, hair removal, pharmaceutical compounds, active cosmetics, fat-sucking devices, muscle-freezing toxins such as Botox, wrinkle "fillers", and breast implants; this culture is willing to pay to change. People would rather pay hundreds and thousands to no longer see or be seen in a particular way. However, some people are never pleased. They ultimately end up with long term physical and mental damage, because of the amount of alterations that have ruptured the skin, tissue and even bones, beyond physical repair.

As if that's not bad enough, a recent report on BBC London (Oct 2020) titled 'Our skin is for life, not for likes', detailed how filters on Snapchat, Instagram and other online apps, are damaging this current generations sense of self and beauty. It's creating images of perfectionism and bringing out major body insecurities. It was reported that Facelift and PlasticaSK to name a few, are creating such virtual versions of self through filters, that many people are unhappy with the real version of themselves without the flawless skin, big lips, skin colours and smaller waists.

There's something wrong, when society has come to accept almost every aspect of human condition, except for the most natural one. Many organisations, such as Mind, the Dove Self-esteem project, and the BeReal campaign UK, are doing their best to promote a body confident nation without filters.

I believe we can all do more to change attitudes to body image, and bring back health to appearance. And it is necessary. But, 'why do people want to be like someone else?' Why has this generation become consumed with presenting imitations of perfection, copying others, behaving like them, speaking like them and even copying the activities of others? Is it just intrigue and admiration, or is it something more? Could it be that people are dissatisfied with who they really are?

Despite the likes, changes, body alterations and recognition from followers, reports are coming out by the dozen, detailing the brokenness behind the pictures.

The Pew Research Centre reported, that we have higher rates of depression than any other generation' (Business insider) They mentioned that 'deaths of despair' are on the rise, as many suffer from loneliness, money stress and burnout at work',(2019)

A Blue Cross Blue Shield report, from (2019) reported that there has been a behavioural health decline in upticks like 'Depression, substance abuse and hyperactivity'.

Furthermore, in a report published last year by Stanford Centre (2019) they reported that more millennials are dying from suicides, with mortality rates increasingly higher now, than in previous generations.

You see the crisis that our world is in, affects you and I. Some of you reading this may be silently whispering this is me too, but I can't tell anyone. It may not be drugs, suicide, money stress, burnout, despair, sexual identity, anxiety or depression, but it may be something else that's loitering beneath the surface.

Even as I continued in my emergence, I had to really reflect on my challenges with loneliness. I don't mean being by myself, no I'm talking about the loneliness that arises from feeling alone with my own struggles, my own deep inner challenges. I had to recognise the shame that was attached to my own feelings, especially in a radical, feminist, be strong all day long, modern culture. You see I wasn't always strong, and at times I would feel vulnerable and weak. Sometimes it made me self-conscious, because I wasn't living up the image of strength I so often saw.

The loneliness was found in my own lack of accomplishment, the loneliness of defeat when I would fall short, the loneliness of my own mistrust of others. I just didn't know who to speak to, I didn't want to be judged. However, I remember sitting one afternoon on my own, and I heard deep in my spirit that I needed to sit down and share my story. 'With who?' I thought. 'With me', was the reply. I sat that day in my room, wandered through the house, into the dining room, and then back again, as I went through each detail of my life from my earliest childhood memory until the present day. As I did, I went through so many emotions, joy, sadness, tears, frustrations and peace. I noted the parts that still brought pain, I even prayed for people as I spoke through painful circumstances, and eventually I pushed through to the end. I realised how many cycles and repeated choices I had made in my life. This process of reflection allowed me to uncover the roots of my own struggles, and to invite deeper restoration and deeper healing into my own life.

For some of you, it may be the pain of insecurities, past abuse, rejections, a divorce, adultery, low self-esteem, an abortion or self–harming, to name a few. But I want to encourage you, be open with God and others who you can trust with your life story. Step away from the cover-up, and allow the inner healing to take form in your life.

It's time to uncover the blockages and to pray that the Holy Spirit will guide you through it. You are not alone and I want you to know that! In fact, I have found that many people actually crave to be naked and real with people, they just find it hard to speak to someone, that they can trust with their flaws without being judged and cast aside. So, some fall into the world's game of living pretentiously, and only showing their strengths.

Some of you may live with the notion, that if no-one else is speaking openly about feeling like you do, there's a good chance you're doing something wrong. But there is nothing new under the sun. There is no challenge that you will ever undergo, that someone-else has not been affected by. That doesn't undermine how you feel, the trauma or pain, but to be whole requires a level of vulnerability.

The power of vulnerability

'Vulnerability, is the risk to expose
yourself emotionally, as you connect with
God and others. It can be very
uncomfortable'.

The original nakedness can be found in the bible, with the famous individuals Adam and Eve. They wandered Eden naked and unashamed in the garden. I mean, the naturalists would've loved it! Everything was exposed. It was the Edenic model, and it was perfect (Gen 2). However, this perfection was destroyed, when they fell into sin, eating of the forbidden fruit, and we have been covering ourselves up with all types of 'fig leaves' ever since.

Being naked can be deeply uncomfortable. Simply looking at your flaws and acknowledging that you have them is a hard feat for most! Yet, it is a great emancipation to the soul, when you can rid yourself of the false opinions you hold about yourself, and be frank with your frailties. I don't mean taking off your clothes and parading around, no. I mean speaking with God or with others you trust, and sharing some of those weaknesses with them, not with everyone.

Confessing sensitive information with the wrong people is self-destructive. Certain details of our lives should be restrained for particular audiences, but make sure you have an audience be it one or more.

Vulnerability seems to make people feel weak. In fact, it has been through my own process of emerging, that I realised how uncomfortable I am, with sharing my own weaknesses. However, I found that conversation after conversation, I would share my own vulnerabilities quite naturally. This was strange because I am usually guarded when it comes to sharing my private life, especially with people I don't know. It's like airing your dirty laundry except people who hear, have the power to throw it back, exploit or control you! However, over the years I have seen the true liberty that has taken place in my life, and in the lives of others, as I have learnt to be open, and to share my humanity with those I've spoken to.

I began to see the power of how our personal struggles, offer a level of credibility and connection with others. They too, can be transformed as they hear how you made it through.

But I want to lend a word of caution. If there is any point where you feel that sharing your information, is to gain a level of interest, shock or amazement. If you're looking for people to say 'how awful', 'how terrible', then you need to fall back! You're not ready yet, and your sharing could do more damage than good to yourself and to others.

You're not sharing to gain woes from your lows, but to share the heights in your fights!

Be a student in life, that is not afraid to open the 'necessary' chapters of your story. Stand as an honest, living witness of grace and strength, to those who are still on that journey! As you share with others, you can liberate those who listen, and break them out of the: 'I'm the only one feeling and going through this' complex. So don't be afraid to be naked, in front of the right crowd and:

> 'Tell the parts you remember,
> Tell the parts you've healed from,
> Tell the parts where you were a victim and
> Tell the parts of your story.
> Tell the parts that caused you shame,
> Tell the parts that changed your name,
> All the parts are just the same,
> It's the power of your story'

Dis- owning your story

Some of you will read this and still say, no not me. I do need time in the dressing room, lets run to the merge part, I'm fine, it's everyone else that has the problem! Look, you may not be ready to uncover the brokenness within you. Your childhood may have been littered with comments, that have always seen vulnerability as a sign of weakness. You may have learnt to be strong at all times, to be resilient to the pain, whilst navigating through the troubled times in your life. For years, you've held back the tears and talked yourself into a crippling silence, instead of crying out to God. Maybe you can't hear the inner cry anymore, maybe you've become numb to the need for healing. The problem is, that it can cause you to disown your story, through a form of self-deception.

> *The most painful transformational journeys are the ones you don't believe you need*

Though it can be hard to identify, the biblical story of David depicts self-deception. I nearly missed it! As King, David was in a pious and respectable position, but he abused his power. He slept with Uriah's wife Bathsheba, and she fell pregnant. To cover up his actions, he ordered that one of his footmen, a faithful man called Uriah, be moved to the front-line of a battle, where he arranged for him to be killed. Then Nathan, a known prophet, comes to him with an allegory about a man who has many lambs, and is rich, but takes the only tender lamb from a poor man. He asks David to decide what should happen to the rich man, and David's reply is that he deserves to die. Nathan said 'you are that man!'.

Yikes! Can you imagine David's face?!

Let's look at his story: David was a man of war, he knew bloodshed even as a child, he witnessed decapitated bodies and those he called comrades never returned home. He killed many (1 Sam 18:7) in fact tens of thousands. Blood was on his hands. Whilst it would be easy to judge David's behaviour in killing Uriah, it is known that there can arise an immunity to self-awareness, when your natural instinct to a threat is survival.

When David was threatened in his first battle as a child, his response was to kill Goliath with a stone and a slingshot. When he was threatened on the battlefield, his response was to kill them. Arguably, David was threatened by Uriah's return, especially because he had slept with his wife, and impregnated her. His natural instinct was to kill. You may say why didn't he kill Saul when he knew that earlier in his life, Saul wanted his life?

Research done by PNAS (2011) show that 'self-deception weighs up the psychological benefit and the longer-term costs'.

The benefit of killing Uriah, one man, outweighed the low cost that he would be found out, and called to account. High benefit, low cost. Whereas the cost of killing Saul, was greater than the benefits. He stood to lose a friendship with Jonathan, he knew Saul was chosen by God, and because of Saul's command, many men and attendants, were already after David's life. I believe that David had developed feelings that would exert unconscious control when he felt threatened, but It had become a part of his nature.

Now, I'm no lawyer, and I'm not standing in his defence, I am simply drawing the historical evidence.

There were no royal garments or anointing that could hide the internal casualties caused by the wars he had fought

You can't afford to remain a casualty of your past, so blinded by your own pain, shame and guilt, that you cast judgement on other behaviours but can't see your own.

David failed to do justice to the facts of his own situation, whilst remaining committed to the values when it came to someone-else's life. Some would say, it was sheer hypocrisy! He did however, confess his wrongdoings, which allowed the remorse and deep inner work to begin. (Psa 51, Psa 32)

All deception, no matter how big or small, can have painful and destructive results in your life, and in your relationships with others and God. Sometimes it's birthed from a place of avoidance of true feelings, or to justify behaviours. Others use it as a defence mechanism to maintain a false sense of control and power over situations. But the best approach to acknowledging the areas that need deep transformation, when you can't see it, is to have Nathans.

Where are the Nathans?

Nathan was not intimidated by David's position, anointing or title, and called him out on his behaviour. He allowed him to see his own wrongdoings and he didn't stutter.

In a culture where everyone is propping everyone up, you need Nathans. Okay ladies, let's call them Natalia's. They are the people who are involved in your life, and help you reflect from an honest place, even at their own personal risk.

They are the communities, friends, families and mentors who aren't afraid to speak the truth, and help you to recognise the cycles, patterns and behaviours, hindering your emergence. They help you to consider what you otherwise wouldn't.

Moving forward intentionally, means some of you need to select people in your circle, and give them permission to be a Nathan in your life, to show you who you are when you've become blinded to it.

Emerging requires you to examine the poor behaviours, and choices in your life, as well as the good ones. You must master holding you, the final product in mind. Gain knowledge about you. Why in spite of your vision and calling, have you lingered in limiting behaviours? What traction invites the appetite to the rough, the rugged, the cheaters, the habits, the low level thinking, the lack of discipline? Behind every choice and behaviour is a need, what need is driving the negative behaviours or has driven them in the past?

There's nothing wrong with needs, we all have them, you just have to discover what your needs are, and determine whether those are healthy or healthy needs.

Is there a void from childhood that causes you to seek attention from all who offer it, a broken marriage that damaged your self-esteem, an abuse you've never shared or trauma, that still leaves you broken? Don't suffer in silence, because there is no need in life that God cannot satisfy. Gift your life with the healing that God can bring. Maybe the knocking is Gods way of asking you to seek help, support, counsel and restoration?

At times, you may feel like I've got past this, but there may be residue.

Removing the last of an old garment

> 'Old wounds can create deep uncertainty, depressions, fears, and avoidances. They may play out in your current feelings, and experiences, but they are really based in the past. They can influence your attraction to familiar figures, or create current conflict, that is really more about unresolved hurt.'

I grew up with a logical, well humoured father and a compassionate and creative mother. Both championed the best in me. I was taught the rich value of loving others and my family. But when I was 18, my heart was broken as my parents got divorced. It was something I never imagined would happen.

For me, it fractured something deep in my core. I seemed to be on a pursuit to mend people. This may have been driven by my inability to mend my parents broken marriage, so many years before!

As I went through life, I thought I trusted God for my own relationships, but cracks began to show in my faith. My thoughts would be taunted with the fear, that any future guy would be unfaithful and disappoint me. I realised that my mind was always waiting for someone to exploit that trust. I was literally looking for the evidence, so I could get out before it had really begun. That way I wouldn't be disappointed or broken. The reality was that the broken pieces remained, and as long as they did, any relationship that was built on that broken foundation, would eventually fail, and they all did. In two of my relationships, the guy found someone-else, and the other dissolved over a period of time.

God began a deep healing which came in phases and seasons of my adult life, and finally ended through my emergence. A lot of healing was brought through a lot of tears, prayer and reading of God's word in my Dressing Room. This process allowed me to see my own flaws, to hold my life up to Gods standard, and recognise where I was coming up short!

There were times I felt like quitting on God. These changes are too hard; I would tell myself! I had so much fear and anxiety built up on the inside, that I felt like it was ready to tear through my clothes like Hulk!

After a few weeks, okay, okay… months. I went from quitting on God to surrendering to the process, with a lot of tears, and saying 'I choose to begin a journey of deepening my trust, transforming my thinking and healing my heart'. It was like being back at the beginning of my faith walk, because I had said all of this at the start, but it wasn't, I was near the end of a process.

I knew that I wasn't going to receive the healing I needed from anywhere-else, and I would not be whole in that area until I said 'yes' to completing my time in the dressing room with God. He wanted to *'heal my broken heart and bind up my wounds'* (Ps 147:3) I had surrendered my heart to the Lord, and I wanted to trust Him with this area of my life again.

Though he tested me, and still does, I know He is just trying to get me to a place of perfect love – without fear. And I'm pretty good at it now! I've spent the last few years no longer looking for men to mend, and I completely trust Gods choice and plan.

Healing is a journey

Healing is a journey and not a destination. Sometimes you can be delivered from the pain, the spirit, the issue, but the residue that is left behind, can take years to heal. Residue is not a reflection that you have not been healed, but it's part of the aftercare programme in your life. It's the deep work needed in your character, activities, choices and behaviours that are still limited and influenced by the past!

You may be reading this now and thinking yes, there are thoughts I still fight with, feelings I still have, bitter memories I have struggled with all my life. That recognition, is where true healing can begin. But, your will power alone, won't get you there. Yes, you need to be open, honest, reflective, prayerful and committed, but you also need the Holy Spirit. It is the Spirit that helps you to take on a new nature.

No person you meet, drink or drug you take, busyness you consume yourself in or church activities you attend, can remove your barriers, alter your character and mend your hearts. You need God's higher power to be your guiding force. That power is the Holy spirit, dwelling on the inside of you, but He doesn't force change. He doesn't drive or drag you into God's plan, instead He leads you, and you must be sensitive to that leading.

Some of you may require counselling, in order to find clarity and speak openly, concerning the areas where you've been stuck in life, don't ignore it. Seek out trusted and recommended counsellors, that can help you to see the roots to some behaviours and actions.

Are you ready to set aside some time, to reflect and pray about areas that need work in your life? Are you ready to have regular and honest conversations about the areas you need to change?

Can I challenge you to have a gentle talk with the Holy Spirit the counsellor, and to go through your life story from beginning to end? As you do, you will find some things still uncomfortable, some may make you cry, and others you may completely jump over. Take a note of those areas, and begin to pray for Gods healing virtue to flow. Ask the Holy Spirit to be your guide, as you remove old garments of pain, sorrow, mourning and hurt, and put on garments of strength, healing, love, wholeness and peace.

Gather your Nathans, you're going to need for the journey!

Finally, let me tell you what the five steps to healing gurus won't.

Deep change will not be easy at all, because *'the mind is hostile towards God'* (Rom 8:7). This means that the mind is in disagreement and opposes the Spirit that wants to liberate you. At times, your mind is going to try and keep you out of the Dressing Room, telling you all types of things. But, the Dressing Room is this place of psychological negotiation, between where you are and where you desire to be. Who you are and who you want to become. This internal debate between the old mind and the new information is deeply real. You will have to learn to keep reminding yourself of why you are choosing to change, and to commit to deep spiritual growth and prayer. A healthy adjustment takes time, so be committed to daily healing.

'Put off the old man.... And put on the new man.' (Ephesians 4:22).

CHAPTER FOUR

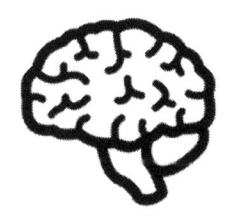

Core – Intellectual Humility

'I originally said no. After reading the script I recognised the role and felt it was a great role... but for someone-else. However, over time I felt drawn to the compelling need to transform and so I accepted'.

(OWN 2012)

I REMEMBER watching an interview with Daniel Day Lewis and Oprah Winfrey on OWN. She enquired about how he prepared to take on the incredible role of Abraham Lincoln. In the film, 'Lincoln', Americas 16th president strives to abolish slavery and reunite his country after the civil war. It was a major feat to play such a renowned character, but Daniel Day Lewis nailed it!

That interview has lingered with me, because whilst he was sitting in that chair looking at Oprah gracefully; I was on my feet in my living room thousands of miles away saying: 'speak my brother, speak!'. This guy was in my living room, not literally, but figuratively.

I too was plagued with similar thoughts. The more that God was speaking to me about the call to work with women, was the more that everything inside of me of was saying, 'who me?!'.

Although I was aware that were some areas of my character that needed work, I also had some of my own self-ideals about the type of woman I wanted to be. And isn't that the case for some of you? The 'self-ideal' has you desiring to be sexy, smart, humoured and strong, or maybe you want to be rough, lusted after, angry, charming or hidden. You may laugh, but what is your self-ideal?

*Oftentimes the character you want to be,
isn't always in Gods script!*

The script is asking for greater: love, joy, peace, long suffering, kindness, goodness, faithfulness, meekness and temperance (Gal 5). Most of these qualities are not celebrated on your television screens, magazines and media outlets. Instead you're bombarded with a lot of films and shows that portray people as vain, backstabbing, cheating, liars, violent and angry. Yes, you may have the odd story of romance, compassion and survival, but it's not the dominant image on your screens.

I know that modern culture promotes and pulls you towards these images and personalities, but some of you need to make sure you aren't embracing these ideals for yourself. Truth be told, some of you like your hard edge, your ability to curse people out who do bad to you. You enjoy your seductive ways and charm, because its drawn particular people into your life. You have mastered the disguise as a manipulator, because its gained you a particular position. And some of you enjoy the feast of attention you gain, from being super loud and abrasive.

I'm not here to judge you, but I am here to make you conscious, that there may be some character traits that you aren't willing to change, and this can create tensions in life's journey. It could be that you think the call to lead a charity serving abused children, looks better on someone who has greater compassion. Maybe the call to relocate to France as a manager of a business company, looks better on someone who is more experienced, and has better self-control when things don't go their way. Or maybe in your view, the call to depart as a leader of your church and to venture into a new local community project, looks better on someone who is kinder and patient with people. And that's the problem, some of you may be perceiving the call, as threatening to the inner harmony you are trying to maintain.

What God's calling many of you to do throughout your life, requires a great submission and obedience, as you emerge with new character qualities. It's not about satisfying your ego, or playing to your pride, but enduring the change necessary to bring a greater level of service.

> *Character commitment is a dedication to a life beyond the one you currently live, and the person you currently are. It drives what you do more than the goals on your list in January, and greater than the vision boards some of you create for inspiration.*

This level of renewal is challenging, because any change, small or large to your character, will require you departing from who you are now, to become someone new. That alone, can feel like you are betraying the person you have known yourself to be. The way you act, your attitudes, morals and choices may all need radical change. However, you will only change when you realise that the person you have been up until this point, no longer satisfies the individual that you are called to be. You alone must 'recognise' the need for character change, and once you arrive at this point, be willing to actually do something about it. Do you feel the *'need to transform?'*, or have you 'quit' in the journey towards inner growth with the confession, 'this is just who I am' (whilst shrugging shoulders).

Giving the impression that you are a completed work and people should accept you just the way you are, is fine for you. But consider this truth, people don't have to accept you for who you are. They don't have to offer you the position, be around you, invite you to dinners, want to be in a relationship with you or offer you that loan. People don't 'have' to do anything.

> *Please realise that conceding to a place of arrival in who you are, diminishes your sense of responsibility to transform (drops mic)*

Taking responsibility

The proverb says:

> *'He who conquers his own soul (the land within) is better than he who conquers the city (the land beyond)'. (Proverbs 16:32)*

This verse came alive for me one night.

I remember going to bed after a long day. It had been an empty day aside from teaching. I had spent a lot of time on my own, and I was reflecting on the journey. I reached to grab my gold bible case and whilst sipping tea, I felt led to read Joshua 17. As I read the scripture my eyes focused on verse 12 - 14:

> 'Yet the children of Manasseh could not drive out the inhabitants of those cities; but the Canaanites would dwell in that land. Yet it came to pass, when the children of Israel were waxen strong, that they put the Canaanites to tribute; but they did not drive them out. And the children of Joseph said why have you given me but one lot and one portion to inherit?'

As I read it several times, I sat up and said, 'Lord we've got it all wrong!'. Like a floodlight path at night, the truth was starring me in the face. I was asking myself 'how Joshua was able to request more land, possessions and blessings, and be given it, when he was still living with his enemies?'. If he had defeated his enemies, surely he would have more land to occupy.

As I lay there re-reading the verse, it became clear that you can be given possessions, promises and land to occupy, and at times God won't hold back His hand. However, nothing you acquire beyond you, is a reflection that you have been purged within. I sat there shaking my head and I began to pray. I asked God to help me look within, and to be conscious of the enemies that I was co-habiting with. I sat for some time really thinking about the character qualities I needed to change, and I began to pray and invite the Spirit of God to do deeper inner transformation. I wanted to be whole and commit to character growth, more than I wanted to acquire anything beyond me.

In the famous words of Michael Josephus:

> 'Good character is more important than wealth, good looks, popularity and even education. These things do not guarantee happiness and often they become obstacles to developing good character'.

Some of you have been experiencing an inner crisis for years. You've been working the job, married, in ministry, prospering and serving the family; you're loved, liked and some even celebrated by the world beyond you, but your commitment to character growth has been poor.

I know it's not easy to confess where you are flawed, but oftentimes the version of yourself that you want to believe is not always accurate, and each of us want to believe our own press! However, this is the call for change. It's time to be brutally honest with yourself, and to stop making excuses for the way you behave.

For some, your character has been your Achilles heel for years. It's the nature in you that when exposed, always lands you in trouble. For others it's your impatience that leads you to always make drastic and poor decisions, time and time again. Maybe it's the need to control others, be devious, jealous, envious, lustful, hostile, dishonest or disrespectful to name a few.

We all have areas in our character we need to work on, and its time you identified yours.

At times you will experience barriers that can prevent you from seeing yourself accurately. It could be arising from those friends, colleagues and circles that have a fondness for your darker 'deviant' nature. You may feel at home amongst them because they are not challenging you to change, they may be just as vain, lustful, controlling, deceitful, unfaithful, unkind or judgemental as you are. And that my brother or sister, is a hard bullet to bite. You may argue that no-ones perfect, and I agree, but character growth is key. You have to push forward with the desire to change; because no-one can give that to you, you have to want that for yourself.

Unless you possess the positive traits in your character for your callings, you will be disempowered to 'fully embrace' the roles and higher service you are called for.

Consider asking those closest to you what they think the three strengths are in your character, and the three areas they feel you could positively change? You may be surprised by what they say, but at least it's a great starting place to begin in prayer and deep inner work. Hold their impressions against the Character qualities in Galatians 5:22-23, and see how you fare. Don't push away the opportunity for great relationships and higher service, because you won't commit to character change. Don't let your pride get in the way!

Pride is not prejudice it comes for everyone!

More often than not, it's your own pride that causes you *to* resist change, or to become resentful when it happens. Pride can function in many ways, but there are two that I believe are most harmful: Self-pride and Intellectual pride.

In modern culture, self-pride is concerned with the self-conscious emotion. Research has suggested that it arises from social comparisons (Smith and Lobel) which usually results in self–inflation (Roseman). You may call it puffed-up-ness! This makes you feel as though there's a need for you to be elevated above others, and this attitude will always war against the Spirit. Whilst pride is probing self-promotion, the Spirit is seeking your humility *in order to be exalted (Matthew 23:12)*

I know men and women who are incredibly gifted, called and anointed, but have been seduced by arrogance and pride with lofty ideas of who they think they are. They must be treated a particular way, given special privileges and always acknowledged. Are you like this? Do you feel that you ought to be recognised more than others? Or do you feel as though you are missing out on something because you are not celebrated? Asking yourself these real questions helps you to uncover why you sense your value is any more than the next person.

The life of Nelson Mandela, has become one of my personal inspirations as his life reminds me to always remain humble. He graced history with a winning combination of charisma and old fashioned courtesy. He was a man who felt a compelling calling, and answered that call with radical humility. He took the path which shaped the humble character that he is remembered by. He rose to fame through painful persecution, physically, mentally, emotionally and spiritually.

During one afternoon, I remember watching an interview on the Oprah Winfrey Network with Nelson Mandela. He was asked how his character had stood the test of time. Dressed casually, with the faint grey in his eyes and hands either side of the chair, he uttered these words to the screen calmly:

> 'You have a limited stay on the earth, you have to reject all negative versions and focus on the positive ones. You have to destroy the myth that you are something more than any ordinary human being. Humility is one of the most important qualities you can ever have'.
>
> (OWN 2013)

These are incredible words, spoken by a man who lived a life that re-shaped the liberation movement in South Africa. He removed himself from becoming inaccessible, mythologised or de-humanised. He was no hero in his eyes, though many South Africans would disagree. He was an incredible man, who was not afraid to *'empty himself' of* any information that hindered his character and growth - liberating himself from pride!

You see self-pride will become an enemy to your destiny, should it gain a firm grip. And in this self-indulgent culture, it has become a great enemy to character progression (James 4:6) Many of you are getting lost in over amplifying your own achievements, whilst looking for recognition, likes and affirmations. But you don't have to brag about simple accomplishments, and constantly communicate 'the good' in what you do, whilst never recognising your flaws. At times, I too have had to be conscious of this, because modern culture will have you focused on your projected self, rather than your inner self. This leads you to keep pumping out captions, images, blogs and videos that present your ideal-self to others. This can blind you from recognising the need for character change, as you start believing that the image you're creating, is actually who you are. This is dangerous, and you must be aware of this in the journey.

Remaining sober and honest in view of yourself, is paramount. But the reality is that pride has a friend called Intellect, and if they both dominate your life, it will be hard for you to rise as high as your spiritual condition allows. 'Intellectual who?' I hear you say. Let me introduce you.

Intellectual pride will keep you from submitting to a greater calling, by amplifying the knowledge and information you already hold, about yourself and your life.

It keeps you from letting go of what you think you know.

Intellectual pride is not new, it is biblical. In Genesis 3, Adam and Eve chose to eat from the tree of knowledge of good and evil. They were told that as they ate of the fruit their eyes would be opened, and they would become like God. They ate the fruit of knowledge, and dismissed the truth and instruction that came from God.

Even today, the attraction and seduction of human knowledge and intellectual advancement, are luring so many away. In fact, many New Age philosophies have built their foundations on the fruit of knowledge. But to each of you there is the challenge to not become lofty and prideful based on the information you hold. Be careful, that you don't elevate knowledge above the word of God, because I believe it's one of the easiest ways to *'fall'* from the new pathway before you.

Please don't misunderstand. Intellectual pride can manifest in your life ever so subtly, by heightening the pride associated with the knowledge of who you are now, your accomplishments and reputation. This leads you to dismiss any new instructions, and prevents you from believing there's an alternative or better view of yourself, your future and God, beyond the one you hold. It has also been known to heighten the feeling that changing could damage what 'you have fought' so hard to accomplish or to build, as if it has been your activity, that has established where you are and who you are.

> *As long as intellectual pride continues to be your defence, to magnify your current accomplishments and successes, you will find it incredibly hard to see the need for greater transformation.*

> *You have to recognise the limits of your own perspective, no matter the season.*

You are not 'all knowing', but God is, which is why He is called the omniscient one. So the view you hold of yourself is only based on the information, character traits and experiences you've had. Therefore, you only view yourself in part, because you lack the revelation to see all the details of who you really are beyond the present moment. Once you recognise this, you can accept that whatever information you hold right now, is inferior to anything God is trying to show you through this transformation.

> *'Don't let intellectual pride disconnect you
> from the more God has for you'.*

Your constant denial of the need to be open or to endure deep internal change, may be good reason why some of you are asking for more from life, but you haven't received it. You don't want to hear anything new if it betrays your self-ideal, or the information associated with who you think you are! But let me tell you what that looks like. It's like going for an interview, and the interviewer asks you if you want feedback on how you can improve, and you say no. The following week you're back in front of the same panel going for the same role, and they are still telling you no. And guess why you can't progress, because you're not open to receive the knowledge that you need about yourself, in order to direct your next steps.

In order to change, it will require deep work to pull up the roots of some character qualities that are betraying you! Your prayer and activity must be driven in a constant commitment to renewal of mind, because it's your mind that houses renewal. The way you think affects the way you behave and what you do. (Pro 23:7) Being honest as you reflect on your character, requires you to ask yourself what you actually believe about yourself and your future. Has it changed over the last few years? Or are you rejecting new information that God has revealed about your path as untrue, because of the deeper inner work it will require? Don't bury your potential in intellectual pride, instead learn intellectual-humility.

Core

Intellectual Humility

Maybe you need a little intellectual humility. I did!

If I'm honest, it was only during my own emergence that I really learnt about it. I hadn't heard about intellectual humility, just humility.

Most of you know humility as the *'freedom from pride or arrogance: the quality or state of being humble'* (Merriam Webster). *It* forms the anecdote to pride and intellectual-pride, as you are free from comparison with others and liberated from a false sense of knowing.

Intellectual humility, on the other hand, takes it a step further. 2 Peter 1:6 calls it 'knowledge temperance', which suggests a level of restraint concerning what you know, and Peter goes further to suggest that, he that lacketh these things *'is blind and cannot see afar off'* (verse 9).

We could stop there, that was a whole sermon!

In essence, intellectual humility allows you to recognise the limitations of your own knowledge and information. It also postures you to see more about your future and to discover who you are.

As I began to grow in my understanding of intellectual humility, I began to see many biblical examples of this. Job had to be taught intellectual humility when He questioned the sovereignty of God, and God responded with the question: *'where were you when I laid the foundations of the earth, tell me if you have understanding'* (Job 38:41). Ouch! The disciple Simon-Peter also experienced a lesson in intellectual humility, when he professed that he would proclaim Christ and not be offended, only to hear

Jesus reply: *'you're going to deny me three times'* (John 18:15-27) It's an amazing example of how you can think you know yourself and your character, better than God. However, it's in the life of Abraham, that you see intellectual humility demonstrated. Although he held onto the knowledge that he needed to kill his son as an offering, he remained open and humble to hear God. As he did, he received a new instruction that meant his son would live (Gen 17 and 18) And his example opens passages of faith for us all.

Beyond the biblical examples, I had my own passage into intellectual humility. One that I didn't understand at the time, but one that remarkably changed my character and life.

My passage to Intellectual Humility

I remember a point when God was really chiselling at my character. I spent time in prayer and as I did, I became conscious of two areas where I needed to build interior freedom. One was the area of control, and the other was intellectual pride.

The two work as sidekicks, as articles show that *'there is a definite correlation between pride and a controlling nature'*. (Mind Renewal 2007) For some reason I had this inner need that I had to be in control of my life, whilst still reluctantly surrendering to God. I had goals and plans that aligned with my own self-identity. But God knew that in order for me to experience life the way He desired, I would have to break free from pride, and the need to be in control.

I was studying my Masters in Education Policy at a reputable University in London. In that year I had passed two modules and failed two modules. It was made apparent to me, that I would have to retake one of those units again after completing my dissertation.

I was incredibly embarrassed and I felt like a failure, because I knew I wouldn't graduate with the rest of my class. I had a little peace, which was based on the fact that I had prayed before applying for my Masters. I knew for certain that Gods information had led me to pursue this path.

I continued in the journey to complete my final module, which consisted of a dissertation around 15-20,000 words. My essay was already underway and my tutor had remarked that it was gearing up as a first class piece. She was generous with her praise, which encouraged me to push on. But as I did, I found out from my father that my grandmother had become ill, which was devastating news to us all. Although she received medical care, she died a few months later from Cancer.

The months passed but I was crushed. My brokenness didn't show during my usual work, service at church and during social times, but each time I sat to write my dissertation I cried and I wept. I felt a heaviness I can't explain. I felt lost, and I knew there was a deep sorrow on the inside of me. I began to look at my life again and ponder in ways that loss can make you.

The emotional weight and sadness I felt, were conflicting with my focus on study. I decided to pray, but I was reluctant. I knew I was meant to do this course, I'd already been humbled through failing two modules, so what more could God say. Nevertheless, I took to prayer and I heard the Holy Spirit whisper on the inside of me that I should walk away. I was shocked by Gods reply, disappointed with myself, overwhelmed and broken. 'How will I explain my choice to those around me?' I thought.

I walked away from my Masters to the shock of my tutor and everyone-else except my parents who received it with peace. Some said 'don't quit', some said 'go back', but most including my very close friends didn't understand my decision. It made no sense to me, but I knew what I heard.

On valentine's day February 14th, nearly two years after starting my masters, I received a knock at the door. It was a recorded delivery brown envelope with my university stamp at the front. I opened it up. Inside was a letter detailing that I had missed graduation, and behind it was a master's certificate, with the university president and lead tutors signature. I sat in awe. Slowly, I placed the certificate back into the envelope and onto the mantel piece, where it sat for several weeks.

That lesson forever changed my life.

Remain open

Divine moments can arrive in life's journey when you are open. Stay seeking new information concerning what God requires you to do in life. As you submit, these can be character grafting opportunities. These transformational moments are birthed out of intellectual humility, as you surrender to the path God has for you.

At times, you may feel as though you are living in the land of the unknown, a feeling that stirs when you are not in control, but remember that:

> *'.. He is with you all the way, working in you both to will and to do of his good pleasure.' (Phil 2:13)*

My encouragement to you, is to prayerfully let God lead. Let Him humble you again to see who you truly are, the good and the bad. Lessen the hold that you have on the information about yourself and your future, and learn to be open.

Every day, the vision of a greater future is going to place a demand on you to change your character, and you have the 'choice' to embrace change or resist! But remember, without a greater revelation of who you are now and who He is calling you to be, you will find it impossible to emerge into the new!

The Land Beyond

CHAPTER FIVE

Unexpected Change

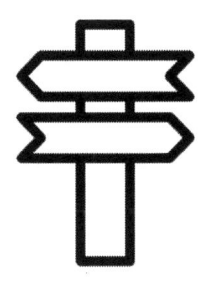

*'Any change, even a change for the better,
is always accompanied by drawbacks and
discomfort'*

Arnold Bennett

AS YOU wait patiently on Gods promises, and on His leading and direction, you will face unexpected changes. Personally, it's one of the hardest lessons I have had to learn in life, to discern what on earth is happening in times of great change.

Have you ever been stuck at points in your life, when you're asking yourself, 'what on earth is going on?', often followed by, 'what's happening in my life…I simply don't get it?'. It can become incredibly hard to make sense of the sudden change, or disruption. It may even feel as if your life is out of control.

Unexpected Change

Unexpected change can benefit your development, because it will challenge you to grow mentally, spiritually, emotionally and physically.

*It can create the disorder that is needed,
to deconstruct the current path, and
construct the new*

For most, it will challenge the way you think and feel, as well as the decisions and choices that you make from that moment forward.

There are three major areas that are tested, during expected change:

- Your emotions
- Your own plans
- Your own conclusions

This is because unexpected change, will always 'force' you to examine the information that's shaped your relationships, activities and the direction for your future. As you try and make sense of the 'unexpected' moments, weighing up what's actually happening, what's changing and what's required of you in your life, you will need 'discernment'.

I grew up hearing the church mothers and fathers, talk about discernment like it was kryptonite. (The stuff you hold against Superman, that emits this radiation and weakens him). They could walk into places, call your name, and start telling you what they were discerning about your life, an atmosphere or a season. They could tell if something was good or bad, by just stepping into the moment, spiritually conscious of what was true.

Discernment means:

> *'the skill of understanding and separating truth from error and right from wrong'*
>
> (Tim Challies)

At times, the skill of understanding arrives though internal or external signs in your life, that need to be sensitively perceived.

This quality is key as you emerge, because life can thrust you into new seasons, that often look opposite to what you expected.

Discernment helps you to seek out the true meaning, so that you can navigate through each season of your life. You have to know when to keep pushing and working on something, and when to find peace with drawing some things to a close.

Discerning through emotion: Your emotions don't always want what is best for you

Oftentimes, your relationships with family, friends, places, spouses and partners will change, as God reconstructs your life. Sometimes it's positive, as unexpected change brings you together, at times it can create distance, as you take on new paths. Knowing who has to stay and who has to go, is essential, but it can also be hard!

I feel a past decision in my own life would provide a better example.

I remember being in a relationship with a Christian guy and good friend, who later became much more. He was very alpha male, tall, dark and handsome. He would cook oftentimes, and he

Unexpected Change

was a good cook! He shared my humour, and if you know me, I love to laugh and we did a lot of that over the years, sharing many moments.

He would try and make time for me between his demanding work schedule, and he worked extremely hard. We stuck it out through family loses, work transitions, personal setbacks, and still held each other's hands, still prayed and believed it could work out.

As we journeyed through the relationship, there were moments where despite his best efforts, I was simply disconnected. I felt as though we were missing something. This lasted a good few months. I just felt that we were going in different directions. Although we would talk about some aspects of the future, I would rarely speak about marriage and commitment with him, and he mentioned that to me some time after we split. Sometimes I wouldn't share my feelings, plans and thoughts with him, because I didn't want to burden him on top of his existing stresses. At other times, I found I was constantly affirming him in his plans, and didn't quite feel like I received the same. There were some levels of support I needed, and encouragement that I often went without, and I learnt that this was okay. However, that feeling of being unfulfilled, wasn't moving. The distance was being created in my heart.

I had become so invested, that despite many dreams God gave me of us not working out, I wasn't ready to let go.

'What if it doesn't get better than this? What if he'll change, maybe this is something I should fight for' - were just some of the questions running through my mind. However, I did end that relationship, and it was really hard because my feelings, emotions and connection with him was very strong.

I felt as though letting go was a sign of admitting defeat, but rather it was me giving consideration to another way, a different way, but not this way.

We came to terms with the fact that we were better as friends. It was hard but I couldn't ignore the internal and external signs, that this was not for me or for him. This also came with the difficulty of me cancelling future plans in my mind, explaining the breakdown of the relationship to friends, and trying to salvage a friendship from what remained with him. Even now, we are friends, though the dynamic is different. I had to accept, that God was leading us down two different paths, and now years down the line, we would both agree God was right.

This may not be your situation, it could be anything from decisions regarding your family, marriage, friendship, positions of people in your company or church, to name a few, but discerning the right decisions and actions is key. Being sensitive to the clear signs, even the red flags, and not ignoring them, will often minimise the frustration that's caused in these season changes!

Knowing when to make your move and when to wait or to let go, can be one of the most defining decisions you make along this part of your life's journey. This is because the soulish parts of yourself, can attach so much sensual and emotional meaning to the various relationships you have, whether it's activities, people, or the constructs you hold about how your future will map out. Hence, the need for change can be rejected. You can find yourself pulling away from the still, quiet voice, that beckons you to move on.

At times you may justify with all the reasons under heaven, why sticking at something you have invested in, should produce a return. Surely God can turn it around. Yes, He can, but His will prevails! Submitting to this truth is hard, because, your emotions can create such bonds with your plans, that it becomes a whole drama of toing and froing, before you can execute clear decisions and choices. This is because:

> *The greatest investment you make in any*
> *plan for your life, is an emotional one*

You may like to think that statement isn't true, but it is. Think about how you feel when you receive an invitation for a wedding, or when you were offered a promotion, or how you feel as you set your yearly plans. Maybe it's the feeling that comes with the prospect of travelling, starting a new project, going to university or college. In each case, the emotional reaction usually swings the door open wide, before anything has happened.

I love this quote from Barclays bank. They said:

> *'Our hearts rather than our heads often have the greatest say in the investment decisions we make, but this approach could potentially harm your long-term returns'.*

This goes to show, that your emotional investment is not only felt in your relationships and activities, but also in your financial plans too.

If your heart leads you in life, the consequences can be damaging. Your heart may reward you with an emotional comfort, excitement, confidence, panic and the gooey feeling you get on the inside. But feelings and emotions change like FTSE 100, daily, or like the wind! It is not a dependent variable to trust, because what you feel isn't always what is true. Just because it feels good, doesn't mean it is good!

> *'Don't let your emotions keep you from making an investment where you will never see a return, or keep you refraining from making an investment because of a past setback'*

Sometimes you are not being asked to move away, but to lean into a situation. To start a new relationship, rebuild a friendship that was broken, trust a husband or wife again who has let you down. But wherever God is leading you through the change, take it to him in prayer.

Spirit over emotion

Learning to be led by the spirit and not your feelings, is evidence of maturity. It is the famous David in the bible, who teaches us to enquire of the Lord and to pray. He demonstrated this at a time of unexpected change, as enemies looted the camp where the women and children remained. This took place whilst he was fighting battles on the front line. David arrived home frustrated, angry and tired, fuelled with emotion, and yet he stopped to pray. He wanted to know if he should chase after what he had lost, the women, the children, and all that had been looted, or let it go. God told him to go after it, to 'pursue it' and recover all (1 Sam 30:8).

With the changes happening in your life, how often do you stop to pray? Are you so angry and frustrated by the feeling of not being in control, that you are not even praying?

Some of you need to seek God's guidance a lot more, because you have spent years making decisions from a place of emotion. That's not to say that what you feel is wrong, many of us battle with overwhelming emotions from day to day. But at times you need to step back, and allow reflection and the Spirit, to consult you louder than your emotional playlist, before proceeding. Learning to push beyond your emotions, rather than ignore them, can richly aid in you discerning the truth of your situation.

It is my prayer, that your discernment would be heightened in this season like never before.

Discerning Opportunity: The plan that manifests when you're over it

There are times when discerning the unexpected change is hard because some opportunities can arise that didn't quite match your own plans and timings.

Some of you live your life looking for new opportunities to show up, like a neon sign that says 'come this way, your perfect destiny awaits'. And yet, most times it simply doesn't arrive like that. Some of you have missed opportunities, year on year, because you can't discern them!

> *Your emergence requires you to see the opportunities God has for you, even when they don't look the way you thought, or don't arrive in the time frames that you desire.*

There are times when things will happen for you, it could be a new job role, work experience, college opportunity or promotion. To everyone else it's great, but for you it may feel like the wrong time, too late, too early, the wrong season, or simply looks nothing like what you prayed for.

You will have opportunities that you need to seize, there's no doubt about that. In order to seize an opportunity, you must discern it. Sometimes it's an obvious opportunity, like a letter in the post, a loan that's confirmed or an offer to a job abroad, and other times it's hidden in plain sight, walking past you in the streets.

I remember attending a well-known church in Baltimore, where the Pastor had declared that 'this week some divine doors were going to open up for people in the room'. (Unfortunately, I had heard these things before!).

That week during lunch break from the Elementary school I was working at, I turned the corner of a sidewalk by the restaurant we had eaten at. My stomach was full of different foods I heaped onto my plate generously - buffet style! As we left, I turned the corner and saw a videographer and reporter in the streets on Capitol Hill. I walked past them whilst they interviewed a guy, and then I remembered the word on Sunday. It hit me in the gut. I quickly turned around, asking my cousin to wait. I walked towards the videographer, a lovely middle aged lady, and said: 'I have studied a BA degree in Broadcast journalism, and I would love to do some work experience'. Even though I said it, I'm not sure I thought anything would really come out of it! (Be careful what you ask for!) The lady gave me a business card and asked me to contact her before the close of the week. I got to my aunt's and showed her the business card, she couldn't believe it! She asked me all the questions under the sun, prying for every detail.

I made contact the day after, and went through several questions with someone from the ABC News recruitment department over the phone. I told them what had happened and that I was told to make contact. I was asked to send an email the same day, and I was given a date and time to be at the News Studio.

Within a week, I was there at the ABC News Channel seven studio. As I approached, I couldn't believe it. I gazed at the moving pictures of the anchors at the front of the building, and as I did my whole body was riddled with anxiety. As I approached I felt incredibly intimidated! 'Wow' I thought, 'I'm actually doing this'. It was an absolute dream come true.

Whilst there, I worked for two weeks in the studios, and worked on the streets developing reports. The reporter and videographer I was assigned to work with, were apparently the top dogs! I met the producers, editors, runners and anchors, who all worked on different floors. It was a labyrinth of technical booths, editing suits, studios, sets and script writers. They all made me feel part of the team. Towards the end of the two weeks, they expressed that they wanted to keep me on. I had a conversation with the producer who asked if I would come back the week after, but I had plans to be in Delaware, at a pre-paid leadership conference. I knew my friend had already gone above and beyond, to welcome and host me.

After meeting the producer, I got back to them over the phone, and declined the offer. Yes, you heard right. I declined the opportunity that I had spent years applying for, that I spent grands studying for, and had even cried over for several years, as I saw rejection letter after rejection letter from ITV, BBC, Bloomberg and Channel five, to name a few.

Needless to say, that decision has stuck with me for years.

I said no, because I didn't plan for it. Suddenly, it was all happening so fast and beyond my control. I was just there to see my cousin, and do some work experience in schools.

The opportunity to stay on at the news station, was surreal. 'How would it work?' I would ask myself. I had so many thoughts, questions and internal debates!

Looking back, there were many life lessons I took from that unexpected moment in Washington DC. But before you indulge in the lessons, I want you to know something. In life, you must be open to revisiting experiences of the past, to ensure that you have truly interpreted all of life's lessons correctly. Why? Because those life lessons become the scaffolding to support your future choices and decisions. The lessons you learn from your past, become the structures for your future. Sometimes, the emotion attached to the moment, can shift your interpretation and meaning. You can see the situation only from one perspective. Looking back at situations in your life, can offer you further insight, as you arrive at new lessons and understanding.

The lessons I had learnt from ABC News Channel 7, were partly around trusting the word I heard, and discerning the opportunity. It was around risk, faith and the willingness to put myself out there. I was fully convinced I had learnt what I needed to from the moment, but as I wrote this book I heard the spirit say 'you missed something'. 'How? I thought. I went back over the sequence, order and timing of those weeks in America, and suddenly as I laid back on my sofa it hit me.

I had always told the story emphasising that it was my zeal and passion for teaching, that caused me to deny the opportunity to stay on at ABC News Channel 7. I had used that to justify my decision all these years. However, as I looked back, I realised that I was seeing what I wanted to see from the experience and maybe that was because I was emotionally invested in my own plans.

As I was led to look back at the same circumstance, I had a new perspective. It became apparent, that throughout the whole experience I didn't seek the opinion of God. Not once. My vision was narrow, and I wasn't open to anything, that took me away from the original reason I thought I travelled to the states. I couldn't see beyond my own plans, and I didn't want to either.

I am not saying that God wouldn't have had me make the same decision, but I didn't even commit to prayer, I went with my plans. So, my advice to you, is put all your decisions on the table, and I mean all of them: work, family, home, ministry, finance and future! Don't make my mistake, at least pray about it or seek wise counsel before making a decision. Without it, you will miss important moments, or make poor decisions about your future.

Unexpected Change

> *Just because you didn't pre-empt the pathway, doesn't mean you aren't meant to walk it.*

The scripture says: '*Where no counsel is, the people fall: but in the multitude of counsellors there is safety*' (Pro 11:14)

If you are challenged in this area, and you know that you can be a bit narrow as you take life's path, ask someone who isn't emotionally invested, to pray with you. Even I have had to lean on the trusted vision of a mentor, to help navigate through unexpected moments of change and opportunity.

When I returned back to London, after three months in the states from Baltimore, to Delaware, to Colorado, Virginia and Washington, I had decisions to make. I felt that I had a deeper connection with my calling and gifting in that classroom with those Elementary school kids, than in the ABC News Channel 7 studios. Something was pulling me back to the children's faces, their stories and their hardships. The children had won my heart, as I connected at a deep level to the abuse, neglect, witnessing of murder and domestic violence, that I had learnt many of these children had faced. They became my children all of them, and they still are. I felt I could bring more change to their lives, than pursuing the career path I thought I loved!

Upon my return to London, I went on to work in several schools and even went further to study a MA in Education Policy.

That unexpected 3-month trip to Washington DC, took me on several unexpected paths, but in the midst of it all, a new path was carved out in education.

I wonder what new paths and opportunities, are waiting for you in the midst of unexpected change?

Open your eyes to the amazing choreography of the unexpected, that can arise in times of change. It's your job to discern, recognise and connect the dots. Let the Spirit lead you. Invite God to help you recognise those moments, to be bold enough to take them when they arrive, and to pass up the plate when you've been denied!

Discerning in the dark: What is clear is not always what is true

Unexpected changes can look despairing, frightening and incredibly bleak! In the natural, the darkened night brings in the day, and you only have to look at Genesis 1:1-3, to see this is true. It details that the Eternal Presence (Spirit), hovered over the darkness of the deep, but He brought a great light, and it was good. The key is, that God *'divided the light from the darkness'* (Gen 1) And that's what you must discern in each season of change, the pathways that have become darkened, and those that the Spirit is illuminating.

You may have begun this journey with deep conviction and enthusiasm, but unexpected change means that, everything that could go wrong, is going wrong! It doesn't feel like a season of new life, new callings or a new day, but it may feel like death. It could be an unexpected financial loss (1 Kings 17:7-16), breakup (Judges 16), divorce (Matt 19:3-9), leaving an opportunity (Neh 1), ill health (Matt 8:1-3), loss of a loved one (Ruth 1, 2 Sam 12) or any other suffering. The darkness can feel isolating, depressing and lonely for some. Whether you are just launching out, or pioneering in your field, whether you are the richest celebrity, or feel like the poorest pauper in the village, no-one is immune from dark seasons.

Dark seasons will always test how deep your roots of faith have grown, it will expose what feeds you, stunts you and grows you. It comes with pain, moments of sadness and a suffering none of you can avoid. The sufferings can cause deep disruptions to your emotions, which can make the right choices and decisions about your faith and future, very hard. But, there are only two decisions in life, you will either choose to walk closer to God or further away.

At times it will be the deep inner conviction that God's is with you, that sustains you even when you can't hear or feel Him.

I remember speaking to a lady who had gone through loss and after loss, and she said to me: *'it was the knowledge that Christ died that kept me, nothing else, I was so crushed.'* It's that real!

Enhancing the time that you spend in God's presence is key, because the worry and anxiety will often try to keep you out. However, it's a test of faith and trust, as He carves out a new road, and I'm no stranger to the pain that can bring. I've had loses in my family with my grandparents, that cut deep like a blade through the flesh. I've suffered heartaches, abuses, anxieties and deep disappointments. But, you have to hope in Him.

You may feel like you are on an island alone, the watchtower light is faint and dwindling, and all appears dark. It may feel as though hope has been sapped from your life, as you struggle to meander through the vortex of disorder, pain and sufferings. However, I want to whisper these words to your spirit, and I just want you to sit still.

> *'This light affliction, which is but for a moment, <u>worketh for you</u>, a far more exceeding and eternal weight of glory'*
> *(2 Cor 4:17)*

It's easy to see the darkness as an inconvenience, an interruption to your schedule and hindrance, but don't prematurely arrive at conclusions about something, that is working for you. No matter how dark the hour of your life may feel, that pain will work for your purpose. The decisions you make, shouldn't be based on what you see, feel and are experiencing. Your decisions have to arrive from a deeper place and conviction.

> *'Because every decision you make in your life, in these moments and beyond, are a reflection of the conclusions you have arrived at about your future'.*

Believing that your situation won't change, you'll never get the job, you'll never see the promise fulfilled, you'll never have children, you'll never live without depression or be happy, are dark thoughts. And you have to take them captive in prayer, before they take you captive. For some, you have become a victim of these thoughts, drinking yourself into a stupor, going back to old destructive lifestyles, using drugs, relying on sex to feel good, to numb you from it all, but you know that won't change the suffering and pain you feel in the long run.

Just consider the chaos of emotion you feel in dark seasons; it's unsettling, but it's another opportunity to lean in and listen, because you need the Spirit of God to navigate you through this change. He alone can help you to discern and know the truth of your situation.

Holding firmly onto your plans, and being driven by the emotion of it all it, can push you into a resistance as you blame God for the suffering that you're experiencing. However, this will only add to the dark cycle of thoughts your experiencing. Instead, read the word and remind yourself of His promises. Seek Him, tears, griefs, shame, guilt and all, because He alone is able to *'give wisdom from His mouth',* along with *'knowledge and understanding'.* (Proverbs 2:6)

You may not get all the answers you need as you pray, but I want you to grab hold of this truth so that you can walk in greater peace:

> *'God doesn't owe you an answer for life's course. Suffering and pain are part of life.'*

This reality, is actually one of the emancipating truths you will hear as you emerge, because you will no longer see dark seasons as an indication that something is wrong with you, it's a rite of passage. What you must determine, is what God requires of you as He leads!

Discerning unexpected moments, requires a willingness to adjust and change. You need to be listening outwardly and inwardly to the Spirit, in order to recognise the clear signs, indicators and shifts. You need to be prayerful about the decisions you make as you move forward in the best way you can. It may be adapting to new relationships, a new normal, a new job, an uncomfortable living environment, or a season of lack, but each change offers you a new perspective.

Don't miss the unexpected opportunities for growth, the hidden moments, the new paths and new lessons, on the other side of unexpected change. As you emerge, remember that:

> *'The person that walks in the fire, out of the storm, and rises about the floods, can be positively different from the person that walked in –it's all about the decisions you make as you pass through it. Be discerning!'*

CHAPTER SIX

The Lost Virtue

I would sit some days, wondering and waiting. Sometimes, it would be on my mind after school as I saw parents, and it would sit in the back of my thoughts at night. Whenever my father was sent abroad, I would miss him. After living in Germany and Cyprus, we didn't travel with him anymore, we remained in London. I would think about what he would be doing out there with the British army. Is he safe? Is he strong? Is he scared? He was never away for too long, but as weeks and months passed, I would do my best to keep trusting he'd be back soon. We all had to be strong. Every night, my brothers and I would pray with my mum for his covering and protection. We would ask God to bring him home alive and without injury. During those times, the strange shaped blue, red and white framed envelopes, kept me hopeful. I would wait anxiously for the postman to deliver the letters, especially when my mother had told us one was on the way. I always knew it was his letter, because of the handwriting at the front, not wildly italic but incredibly beautiful, perfectly on the line with each t crossed, and each i nicely dotted. I would gently open the envelope, because in those days the envelope also formed part of the letter. Each word my father wrote in that letter was like water to my soul, it would realign my trust and quiet my fears. It was as if he was right there with me! He would ask how I was, and remind me I was on his mind and that he loved me very much. Every letter encouraged me to be patient, that my father, the soldier, would be coming home soon. (In 1999 my father was permanently brought home with a promotion and stationed in the UK)

ALTHOUGH THAT experience was many years ago, it is still one of the strongest childhood memories I hold of waiting with expectation, for someone I couldn't see. It sits as a keen reminder to me, that there are lessons and experiences that we carry right from our childhood into our adult lives. These lessons become a reference point as we learn to respond to the world around us.

I wonder what your earliest memory is of having to wait patiently, and what you learnt?

Patience in changing times

Nowadays, access to loved ones rarely happens through letters. The new interface of technology has changed the way most people engage and connect. Information and answers to some of your deepest questions, can be found through a couple of clicks online, in just a few seconds. Even our phone, televisions, computers and household devices are becoming more intelligent, they speak to you, turn off your television, lighting and play music.

Every day, technology is evolving to keep up with the growing demands and fast lives, that define our culture. You can even see the effects of the tech culture, in the next generation of children today. They can spend hours online, on YouTube, gaming and computers, throwing the most dramatic tantrums with major breakdowns, when small things don't go their own way. I am sure that many of you have witnessed this!

The mantra of modern society seems to be that everything must be done quickly, now! Breakthrough, now, answers, now, food, now. The culture of immediacy is altering behaviour and expectations, which in turn can impact your ability to be patient.

Waiting for anything nowadays, is interpreted as a failure of service and a delay.

However, life can be fuelled with real frustrations and struggles that technology can't solve. The demand that everything should happen now and quickly, is not realistic in life. You need patience!

Psychologist Sarah A. Schnitker, created the 3-factor patience scale. She argues in her work that says we all 'need' patience in the following areas:

1. Hardships you experience with others (these are interpersonal, like arguments and disagreements),
2. Daily hassles (like waiting for the cashier at the checkout, or kids to get ready)
3. Serious setbacks (lawsuits, health diagnosis, natural disasters or loss) most of which, technology can't change.

She paints a clear picture that illustrates - patience is key to the way you engage with others and control yourself.

Some of you may be great with daily hassles like being in traffic, waiting for someone to serve you, or waiting for the children to get ready for school, but you may struggle immensely with serious setbacks, that endure over weeks and months. Consider how you behave when you are waiting for an exam result that may take time, waiting for an important answer to a prayer you prayed months ago, waiting for a season of hardship to end, or waiting for a report on your health. How do you behave? Which areas are you least patient?

It's easy to get restless, eager, irritable, frustrated and even nervous in the process when you are waiting for particular things in life to take its course. Before long, you a can find yourself asking: When will things happen for me? When will changes manifest? And when will the situation get better?

Impatience can begin brewing like a tea gathering strength over time, or like a sudden moment where you can't take it anymore, leading to an explosion! It's often fused with sentences like: 'I'm not doing this anymore, I'm done, I'm not serving here, I'm not staying in this relationship, I'm quitting this job' or 'I'm leaving this ministry'. At other times, impatience can manifest in a slow and silent departure from the trust and belief that things will change. This can lead you to make hasty, and often impulsive decisions, as you try to take control of the wheel of your life.

In my experience, impatience arises from your own sense of premature timing. It usually concerns a goal that will take more time than you anticipated, to achieve it. The frustration is caused by the sense of delay on your own timeline. As you look at life's clock with the months and years passing by, you can feel as though you've got to do something to accelerate or create faster change.

*'In times like this, you are not asking to
accept the things you don't know and grace*

to accept the... blah, blah, blah. You want change and you want it now!'

I remember one summer, God was still speaking through many dreams and scriptures, some I understood, some I didn't! At times the information that I received came in pieces, and usually I would be okay with this, except there were some pressing decisions I needed to make regarding my tuition business, as I brought some things to a close. At moments, I felt as though I had a puzzle that came in a box with several pieces missing, that's how it was sold and that's how I bought it. The challenge I had, was that I wanted the rest of the pieces now, and I was praying and even fasting for them. I wanted more details about how I would financially sustain the charity. Should I still continue with home tuition? What happens to all my staff who served with me in the schools, do I let them go? I wanted those answers before I made any further commitments and investments, but I wasn't getting them.

Days and weeks passed, but one night, I had a dream where I walked along a narrow pathway, one side was a brick wall, and on the other side was water as far as I could see. I began to notice an unusual pathway across the water. It looked like two lanes. I dipped my toe in the moving waves, but when I realised my path was going in an unknown direction and I couldn't see where it was leading, I stepped back onto the pavement. I awoke to the revelation, that I wasn't committing to the pathway I needed to tread, or stepping out on faith. But I had good reason, I told myself. The pieces seemed wildly disconnected, how will they all fit together? How can I travel, teach and develop a charity? And why am I having random dreams of other broken women who need healing, whilst doing missions? The answers weren't coming quick enough, and I had the additional stress of making a decision about the work I was doing with my schools. I was praying, but growing deeply impatient, frustrated and fatigued as time went on. It was a

Psalm 10:1 moment, *'Why, Lord, do you stand far off? Why do you hide yourself in times of trouble?'.*

The pressure was rising each day. The more I waited was the more I began to seek and find what little meaning I could, with the clues that I had been given. I was anxiously up at night and frantically thinking throughout the day. It didn't take long for me to start making decisions and choices based on my own wisdom. The more anxious I became was the more I started to lean on my own understanding and past experiences. Before I knew it, I had created my own 'botched' picture of how things will work out. I was overthinking and planning my life with answers that made sense to me. 'Once I've completed this project, that will happen, once I've been to that country and visited those people, this will happen. That piece will slot with the charity there, and they must be coming to support here'.

In all my understanding, I had to concede after a few weeks, yes weeks! That none of my best efforts could piece together the vision of the future, because most of the essential pieces were missing. For Pete's sake!

One beautiful and sunny afternoon, I sat miserably in my garden with my head in my hands. I was mentally and emotionally exhausted, and disappointed. As I sat there, I began to ask myself where all the anxiety was coming from? Why was I living so far ahead of the moment?

I decided to rest and to be still. As I did, I slowly began to pray. The more that I placed my frustrations back in the hands of God, was the more I could feel a resistance. Nevertheless, I prevailed through it and kept sharing my burdens with God. Slowly, I began to experience a refreshing peace and sense of order. Finally, I was enjoying some rest as I sat in the Eternal presence (omniscience) of God. I had stopped worrying, fussing and overthinking, which was opposite to the activity that my mind had me engaged in, throughout the previous weeks. Simply coming back to a place of rest that afternoon, allowed me to realise that the land within me, my spirit and mind, was absolutely exhausted. My own stress and anxiety was sucking dry the little strength that remained. As I remained still, I could sense a lesson arising. I opened my phone to the Bible App, as I felt led to turn to Leviticus 25:4-5. It read:

> *'But the seventh year thou shall be a Sabbath of rest unto the land, a Sabbath for the Lord: thou shalt neither sow thy field, nor prune thy vineyard...for it is a year of rest unto the land'*

My initial response was, 'how does this relate?'

As I researched about why farmers let the land rest, the eyes of my understanding opened wider. I learnt that rest not only allows the soil to regain its natural nutrients, and to be replenished for new seeds, but it also breaks up the cycles of pests and insects, that have nestled their way into the soil.

Whilst sitting there in silence, with the soft breeze blowing, I began mull over the scripture and that's when it hit me.

Resting in God has the power to expose damaging cycles and insects – in essence the things that don't belong in the soil of your life. It could be negative words, activities, thoughts and behaviours that may be hindering your life. If you're open to it, rest can actually posture you to receive new words from God, in the same way that the fertile soil is ready to embrace new seed. I saw in awe again at how Gods word brings new practice and perspective.

I realised that my impatience was counterproductive to my progress, and it was affecting my ability to really connect with any new information. Instead of panicking, I went back through my notepads and revised the words I had already been given. I decided to focus my attention on what was required of me now. Nothing more and nothing less.

As I let the natural course of time play its part, it became clear that I needed to let go of some staff from my tuition business, after many months of keeping them on payroll, but only when their contracts came to end. The rest positioned me to consider new information that came over the weeks, which informed my decision to decline the offer to return to the schools. A few weeks after that, I began to work on the Charity again. I registered for several online programmes and activities that were focused on ending sexual exploitation. Suddenly, event after event was happening in the areas I needed more knowledge. I gained essential research and information in that time, to help me make some structural decisions.

As the weeks went by, I found myself back on course. No longer in an unhealthy panic. But between me and you, I didn't do this without a little bit of kicking and screaming concerning the answers I still wasn't getting. I like to bow out in style with epic moments, and no I'm not encouraging you to do the same.

Although at times you may want to be in control, which is where the impatience is arising from, position yourself in surrender, and let go of the future moment that is beyond your control. Far too many of you are driving yourself into distress, fighting for things that are already promised. Wait for instruction, only then can you be guided wisely.

Patience during serious setbacks

'The hardest lesson God can teach you in life, is that you are not in control'

Impatience isn't always arising from the lack of information or answers. Navigating through life, will reveal that patience is tested greatly during the storms, the disruptions and interruptions. These can be the hardest lessons in life that can rupture your normal as you are thrust into a new path. For some of you, the waiting season is an opportunity to re-prioritise and to re-align, knowing that the instability and catalysts of change in your life, do not hinder, delay or alter God's plans.

God may change your plans, but His remain the same

God is always present, He is always in control, but you must learn to trust that even when you don't understand what is going on. You cannot wish your way through, or force life along with hurriedness. You may feel as though peace hits one area of your life like your family, but then something crazy is happening in your relationships, once that's sorted someone else has a diagnosis of ill health, just as you get through that, your finances are hit with competing demands. It's the kids, the husband, the wife; it's everything and everyone. It can feel like a storm taking your life out of control! But even as some of you go through loss, pain, depressions or frustrations, you must learn to slow down or you will only do damage to your health. Could you be filled with ills, pains, mental health challenges and other afflictions because you won't rest?

A 2013 study, published in the Journal of Abnormal Psychology, explored *'the link of stressful life events to symptoms of depression and anxiety'*. They reported that dwelling on your problems and overthinking on issues increases your risk of ill mental health. The study shows that overthinking actually paralyses your ability to analyse correctly. As you get stuck in your head you can become dragged down with worry which makes it harder to discover real answers and solutions.

In essence, getting frustrated and impatient now, about something that 'may' be beyond your power to escape, that feeling, diagnosis, person or circumstance, will only create more physical, emotional and mental suffering, as you run ahead in your mind looking for a quick solution and over thinking things.

Learn to take one day at a time and stop overthinking - do what needs to be done for the day and live in the moment. Don't live so far beyond yourself for the 'big thing' or 'breakthrough', that you miss the precious gift of life now! The children, those you serve, the little you may have, the roof over your head, the gift of life and salvation. Do not despise these. So many of you could be missing small moments, signs and answers that could bring relief, because you are busy overthinking and wearying yourself, when God wants to give you solutions and rest (Matt 11:28).

Take time to slow down, and use the time wisely. Focus on the key activities for the day, which will allow you to be more productive, than drowning in worry about something beyond your control. Handle what you need to do today, and not tomorrow (Matt 6:34) Trust that the insight and information you hold is reliable, and stay open and flexible to Gods leading. At the right time, you will receive what you need, as you continue to knock, seek and ask through prayer (Matt 7:7-12).

This is your chance to develop the physical and spiritual stamina, the emotional muscle and mind-set, needed for the next part of the journey. See your current challenges as the chance to discover new solutions, to be creative and to find the resolve to reconnect with Gods new rhythm.

During serious setbacks, you must be careful that your impatience is not arising from false expectations about your future, and mistruths that you are holding onto.

The shadow life

'Don't let someone's lips become the snare of your soul' (Proverbs 18:7)

Unfortunately, impatience can arise when people create expectations that aren't in line with Gods word. As you take those words and believe them as truth, it can create impatience, as you long for something you will never have. This can lead you to live the shadow life, where the choices and decisions in your life are being built in the shadows of other people's expectations. It could be false prophesies, false words, or people adding their own opinion of your situation and life, as though it's fact.

It could be that you are concerned about the prospects of your business, you share that with a close friend and they say: 'don't worry, this time next year your business will flourish', when actually Gods using the waiting season to reveal it's going to close down. Meanwhile, you are investing money, time and energy, getting frustrated, as God ends something you think will live. Perhaps you go for a job role and the interview went well, you share that with someone who says: 'go for it, I see you working there already, they're definitely going to call you back tomorrow for the job role, who wouldn't want to hire you', but you wait week after week, never getting the call back from the employer. Actually God has a completely different role for you. Maybe you share that God has called you to start a business with a partner or close friend, which will mean relocating to China, and they respond: 'I hear you, but I just don't believe that God could be saying that, there's no money in outreach with the poor in China. I hear Him saying you've got work to do in the America'. Instead of moving towards where God called you, someone-else's opinion has caused you to abandon what you know is true. Now you're looking for roles in America.

It could be around anything, from work, your ability to have children, a disease, a ministry, spouse or a career prospect. It may not be intended as harmful, but it can cause you to veer off the path and even destroy your own ability to discern God's direction for your life. Sometimes the words are coming from people who love you and care for you, and at other times you may be the author of those false expectations, exerting them on someone-else. But the last thing you want is for you or anyone else, to expend focus, activities and energy, waiting patiently in areas where it isn't required.

Don't miss this, because these snares have hindered some of you in the path to discovering your callings. Remember that:

> *'Unless the LORD builds the house, you are building in vain' (Psalms 127:1)*

That whole business, career, relationship, outreach or ministry will begin to crumble, erode and fall apart, because it was never for you in the first place. So, despite how certain others may sound, be mindful and prayerful that people don't manipulate you, altering your expectations, and causing you to live them out. Learn to test the spiritual nature of others, as to whether they are of God or speaking in truth. Many false prophets, teachers and speakers are in the world. (1 John 4:1-5) I've met a few! However, it can't all be blamed on other people, because sometimes it's you.

I know from experience, that false expectations can be created when you may want to believe the possibility of a particular word, activity, calling, action or situation in the future so much, that you refuse to wait on direction. Your own wants and desires, can lead you in pursuit of people, positions and places in life, which can lure you away from those you are called to serve. It may be the prospect of love, a pay check, recognition, a particular role, or whatever your vice is. Before you know it, you are believing in faith that something will happen with such a certainty, that you begin emotionally and intentionally praying for and expecting it to actually happen. But you can't force Gods hand. Some of these things God never promised to give you in the first place (say it again) Some of these things God never promised to give you in the first place! However, you have embraced them as real, and now you are experiencing deep anger and frustrations, because life hasn't gone the way you expected.

> *False expectations are one of the biggest killers of any modern day relationship, let alone your relationship with God*

It doesn't matter who you are, having an unmet expectation is crushing because you have already made the emotional investment believing it will happen. You can begin living out what you want to happen, before Gods said a word. You've bought the suit for a new job, or the ring for the engagement, you've already started to get excited for the breakthrough in 15 days, and you're already packing your bags for a new house. As far as you're concerned, whatever you desire and want is going to happen. Unfortunately,

> *'There's a fine line between faith and consumed desire'*

Every so often it's healthy to stop and do an inventory on the information you hold. Why are you behaving the way you are? Are your plans and expectations in life, based on what is true? What are the origins of the information you hold? Realistic expectations should be birthed and brought to form through the Spirit of God, His word you can trust with your life.

Some of you may need to rethink the foundations upon which you are building your life. Maybe there are seeds producing fruits of direction, choices and decisions, that are contrary to Gods path for you. I pray it will be revealed in this journey, even during your sleep. When you recognise where you've eared, then pray about it, and wait for Gods answers.

Power in the wait

'It is faith and patience' that allows you to inherit the promises (Heb 6:12) and fulfil the word over your life.

There is great power that is dispensed when you can learn to endure waiting seasons, with aligned expectations. Those words and promises that you carry, keep you as your faith is tested.

When life teaches you patience it can make or break you. Either you're going to survive it and land on the shores of new possibilities and change, or quit and sink back into a place of frustration.

At times, I reflected on how many teachings I had heard on faith and patience, and it was a few. But both are required as you live out your callings in life. In fact, I believe that some of the issues that you think you have with faith and believing God, are actually issues around patience. It's not that some of you don't believe God for your future and callings, but waiting and patience can test the strength of your faith. Caleb knows what I'm talking about. He was the man in the bible who waited for 45 years to inherit the promises of God (Josh 14;10-13)

I say all of this because faith requires patience, and patience means waiting. In essence it will be impossible to ascend to any greater level of faith, without the testing and perfecting of patience in your life. There's no getting out of it, but there is great power in it.

One of the instructions that Jesus gave the disciples before his ascension, was to 'wait for the promise of the father' (Acts 1:4). He knew it would take great wisdom for them to obey these instructions, but he also knew it was key to their service. The bible details that they were all 'in one accord' as they waited on the day of Pentecost, for the promise (Acts 2: 1). They didn't get angry, frustrated or run ahead. Neither did they open the doors and begin ministering to the broken and divided communities around them. No, they were intellectually humble, and knew that there was an endowment and power that they needed, in order to respond to the crisis of the age. They had no knowledge of who or what the Holy Spirit would be, but they trusted the promise of God.

In the same way, you have to trust God as you wait. He alone can strengthen and empower you, as you endure a season that you may not understand. You may have no idea what's on the other side of your patience, but you must find a way to persevere with trust. As you do, I pray that you will begin to see the wait as your friend and not your foe.

As you deepen your understanding of what's required of you, I see you realigning, listening and raising your expectation for the future.

You must recognise that you are at the gate of an airport with a guaranteed ticket for flight. You can't stress over when the plane doors will open, and you're in no position to make the process of boarding happen any faster than it will. But you can choose to wait in expectation, to become strong as you remind yourself of what you heard, what you know and what you believe. The turbulence of life, and the winds of change may challenge you through your transition, but you can trust the pilot of your life. There's no going back now, there are people who need your service on the other side of this.

It's time that *'you who have dwelt in the dust, wake and shout' (Isaiah 26:19)* with renewed strength and patience for the journey. It's time to speak into the *'womb of your morning'* (Psa.110:3) and to prayerfully usher in your divine destiny. I encourage you to set an alarm and awake each day, speaking, affirming and declaring the promises of God. Before your mind is filled with worry for the day, before you look at your phone, take a moment to rest and declare, that there is power in the wait and you won't be denied it.

'Wait for the Lord, be strong and take heart.' (Psalms 27:13-1)

CHAPTER SEVEN

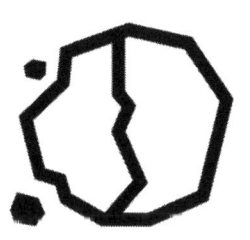

The flint, the diamonds and the compass

*'An emerald is as green as grass; A ruby red as blood; A sapphire shines as blue as heaven; **A flint lies in the mud**. A diamond is a brilliant stone, to catch the world's desire; An opal holds a fiery spark; **But a flint holds fire**.'* Written by Christina Rossetti.

Find your flint

FLINT IS not considered to be attractive due its dark grey, black, green and beige colour. It most certainly doesn't

The flint, the diamonds and the compass

yield the same type of admiration and value in the world as the treasured diamond, which brings with it great wealth. Hence, it is often overlooked and lays lost in the mud of our lives. Yet, flint is the only stone that has the power to produce fire, and can help to sustain you as you journey across new terrains.

The great thing is that you all have flint buried deep on the inside of you. They are the natural talents and abilities you are born with. They are the clues that you already have on the inside of you that are attached to your core. Like DNA, they hold some of the complex details about your make-up.

The common place to start in life, would be to mine your flint, and to discover the unique potential you harness, but the reality is that many don't.

As you grow through nursery, primary school and secondary school, you aren't really taught to look within. and to let the natural wellspring of talent flow. There's no topic or subject that helps you to recognise your natural abilities or talent like: writing, sculpting, advising, singing, leading, comedy and so on.

Instead, most of you spend the first half of your life, hard pressed to look beyond you at the world, and to acquire the skills, and qualifications for your future course. You are told that world of business, politics, the arts, engineering, science, economics, technology and more, are already desiring of different skills and abilities, and you are encouraged to find where you fit in. Don't tarry on it either, by the end of year 9 (age 14) in the UK, you are already told to make key decisions about GCSE pathways you will take, and they should be considered with your career in mind.

There's no doubt that the world seems to be rushing people to make decisions about their future, without real insight and discovery, of your raw talents.

On the contrary, it can be argued that the modern education system has chartered the course towards celebrating those who are 'gifted and talented', with schools adopting new programmes and special privileges for these children. And although that may be true, what have they done to develop the potential in the other children who are still discovering what lies dormant inside?

In 'Finding Your Element', author and educator, Sir Ken Robinson, seems to identify the problem. He describes how our education system has a narrow view of ability and aptitude, based on measuring I.Q. This limits our understanding of ability, as there are many people who have a natural aptitude to fix things, create things, solve things and provide solutions to things. Oftentimes, these qualities are not developed, not encouraged, and marginalised in our system of learning. This affects how you see yourself, and how you fit into the world beyond.

Also, in an article written by Christianity Today on 'Buried Talents' they wrote:

> *'that unless the gifted child is challenged*
> *by proper environments and stimulated by a*
> *specially adapted education, he/she may*
> *never realise his/her capabilities, let alone*
> *make a commensurate contribution to*
> *society'.*

There's no denying that educational environments, such as schools, churches, your homes, and people you spend time with, play an important role in the development of your raw potential. However, beyond the education system, some of you still haven't unearthed your potential. And there may be many reasons for this. Maybe you've been running rampantly in the pursuit of your own intellectual growth and motivation. Or you may have been consumed with chasing the thrill and the wonder of the world lured away by the 'rubies', 'emeralds' and 'sapphires' that you equate with high value, whilst neglecting the inner vault of raw talent, your flint.

Well, this is your sign that it's time to mine.

The miners are rising up

'Millions of people are awakening to mine their flint using what they love or do well'

Modern culture is challenging the world to mine and use their flint. Just look at how YouTube, the multimillion pound social engine, has encouraged people across the world to recognise that they are naturally skilled and talented.

Kevin Allocca, who wrote an article titled: 'How YouTube is Changing the World' (2018), claims that YouTube and Web Entertainment, have caused everyone to recognise, that a professional level of creativity and talent is thriving online. Tomorrow someone will have a total nonsensical idea and turn it into a creative idea – that will turn into something that will touch the lives of millions of people. We all now make that possible.

There's an array of people who don't have the professional skills, qualifications or experience, but lead on areas they are naturally talented in, such as makeup, hair, mechanics, artistry, empowerment talks, baking and teaching. YouTube drives millions of views annually, and makes even more millions, based on the content that's uploaded. Some of these individuals, may never be offered the opportunity to do what they do online in the professional world. However, that's not going to stop them from unleashing their potential, and doing their best to shine the brightest with more and more compelling videos, blogs, articles and posts. It's become a competition of who can attract the most followers, get the most likes and subscribers.

Unfortunately, beneath all of this 'talent', there are many who are copycats or just mimicking the activities they see others do, from preachers, prophets, bloggers, make-up artists and inspirational speakers. Some may put on a sterling performance, because they are good at what they do, but has there been a genuine discovery of their own natural talents and abilities, or are they just following the trend?

Whether you have a presence online through social platforms, such as YouTube, Twitch or IGTV, I want to encourage you to show your true self. Don't mimic what exists because it's fashionable or lucrative, take the step, do the work and mine your own talents and abilities.

It's in the dirt

> 'The parable of the talents tells us, that there were three men who were given talents, 2 men invested their talents and gained an increase on their return. The other man was given a talent too, but rather than invest it, he dug in the earth and buried it' (Matt 25:14-30)

What have you buried in the dirt? And why?
The Harvard Business Review on Talents (2018), reported:

> 'Experts have long encouraged people to play to their strengths. .... But based on observations, this is easier said than done. Not because it's hard to identify what we're

good at. But because we often undervalue what we inherently do well'.

I couldn't agree more! Like anything in life, when you are taught to value something, you handle it differently, protect it and cherish it. Some of you are natural helpers, good teachers, great motivators, or naturally creative. But, do you notice what you do naturally and often get thanked for? You may be seeing them as insignificant, because it comes effortlessly, but it's making a difference in the lives of others. Sometimes, you may even be intentionally majoring in some abilities and talents that you think are more celebrated, like cooking, craft making or designing, and neglecting other talents that are less common or not as celebrated. However, you must remember that your talents aren't just about you, it's about the service you bring to the lives of others.

Are you holding back talents that could bless others richly?

Sometimes, it's the people who have known you the longest, that are best suited to help you identify your talents. Asking a parent who has nurtured you, or a close friend or spouse who has watched you grow, what your natural talents are, can be quite revelatory. As a child you may have played a sport, wrote poems, drawn incredible pictures, painted portraits or designed clothes. It's easy to forget your flint as you mature in life, there are far more serious matters you may feel require your attention. But I want to encourage you that a flickering insight into the past may be telling, you never know what you might discover about yourself.

During my emergence, God had me digging on bended knees in prayer, and with dirty nails, through the rubble of my own life. I had to find the talent I had buried in the dirt!

The flint, the diamonds and the compass

I remember being in Antigua, where I was celebrating my brother's wedding. I remember walking towards the deep blues and dancing turquoise waves of the ocean, and being overwhelmed with such peace and beauty. Tears rolled down my eyes. The sun was like a warm hug around my shoulders and the soft breeze from the ocean was welcoming. I observed nature's beauty, which in an instance, lifted my heart and the weight that I was carrying. The enchanting garden of trees, the Kew Garden styled hedges with unusual flowers, and the pulling of the tide, swept me away!

As night came, I retired to my room after taking in the incredible food, hospitality and activities for the day. I lay in bed listening to the eerie chanting of the waves through the window.

I had been overwhelmed and quite stressed, by the transitions in my life. The business wasn't doing so well, and financially I was struggling. I felt like I was working harder than ever and taking more risks, but with little financial return. Some of you may feel the same at times! I had many important decisions to make, the pressing one being whether I would continue with the business or not. After sitting there in the stillness with thoughts swanning around, I decided to pray on it. I began to ask the Lord for further direction about my life, in a simple and honest prayer. I turned the light off and snuggled into bed. That night I had a strange dream. In the dream, I was standing and holding a book that I had written. Next to me was my current Bishop, who wasn't my Bishop at the time of the dream, because I was at another Church. In the dream, I seemed pleasantly overwhelmed.

The following morning, I wrote the dream down in my notepad and dismissed it. 'Me? Write a book?' In my prayer, book was not a word I used. Family, life, direction and business were the ones I had mentioned. Being overwhelmed, an abstract dream about a book, was the last thing I was going to entertain. I wrote the dream, and left it there. I had no prior professional writing experience, no desire to write a book, and the thought alone of the time and energy it would take to complete, was enough to put me off!

The strange thing is that my mother had told me about pages and pages I would write as a child. She would detail the hours I could spend going from one story to the next. It just came naturally. And although I was cognisant that I had a talent to write, I chose not to use it.

4 years later, I sat one afternoon in January 2019, and returned to my journal to remind myself of the things God had said over the years. I soon realised whilst flicking through the pages, that I had never dug up that flint! I had never written a book. I was lost using the same gifts in the same way, with the same methods. I had missed it completely. God knew I could reach people through a different method and a new talent, but I had to take the limits off of myself.

*Don't let what's familiar hold you back
from discovering what's new*

I decided to return back to the dream and finally put pen to paper, and by April the same year, I had completed the first draft. Here I am now, manifesting the deep unknown and hidden potential of 2015 in 2020.

I know it's incredibly easy to look at any new talent development as an uphill task and a major feat. It takes commitment and a lot of investment, to step out and operate in something new. Even for me, writing is a completely different skill, and has taken a lot of adjustment, tears, screams and at times a lot of learning. I had no confidence that I could actually write a book. However, through prayer and trust I persevered. The Holy Spirit led me all the way, hands down. He even gave me a concept to use as a template, which was based on an actor emerging from training and auditions, to getting their big break on the stage. You'd never believe that that's where this book started! At times, it would have been easy to stop, quit and give up, especially after long sleepless nights and the plague of editing! However, I had to push through. I knew that if God showed me this book in a dream, then there was a lot more connected to finishing the book, than just the book.

In all, I have learnt how to use my teaching gift through written material, as God wrapped my gift up in my talent. This book, has taken me on my own personal journey of restoration and renewal, as I have overcome my own self-doubt and trust in God. Now I am positively enthused, and ready to reach a new audience through a new method.

You may think you've seen all you've got, be flowing in it and using it, but just stop and ask the Holy Spirit to reveal your talents through this journey. If you do, and you sincerely yield to His leading

> 'He will give you the treasures of
> darkness and hidden riches in secret places,
> that you may know that it is HE the Lord that
> calls you by your name '(Isa 45:3).

You are not just being called to serve God greater, you are being equipped for it too.

I wonder what God may be uncovering in you as you pursue the call to others? What natural abilities are stowed away on the inside? What's been undervalued and overlooked? It's time to awaken them again!

You haven't realised it yet, but there is a symbiotic relationship between your flint and your future, because your talent has people's lives attached to it. The same way that you benefit from the use of other people's talents, is the same way others are meant to benefit from yours. You are meant to *'invest'* in what you have, so that you may *'enter in the joy'* that comes from using what you have. That was the what the talent investors received in the parable. *(Matt 25: 14-30)* Discover the joy again, as you invest in using your unique talents in ways that only you can.

For some of you, this is an overdue wakeup call to remind you that each part of your life matters, all of it! You are the manager of the talents that have been given to you, and you have a duty to care for what has been loaned to you whilst you tread the earth. At times, using your talents will earn you money, recognition and fame, but this ought not be the chief premise for using them. Instead, use your flint to ignite little fires in the lives of others, fires of intrigue, fires that draw others towards the light of Christ.

Light those fires!

(Figuratively, for those who just reached for matches and grabbed their boots!!)

The gift

Everyone may have a talent, but everyone does not have a gift. I stress this, because at times the terms talents and gifts are used interchangeably in our modern culture, which has confused many.

'Gifts are like diamonds, they are pure, rare and desired'

'A Spiritual gift is any ability that is empowered by the Holy Spirit and used in any area of calling and service'. (Wayne Grudem, Systematic Theology)

The bible details what these gifts are, such as: teaching, wisdom, faith, healing gifts, miracle, helps, administration, prophecy, distinguishing spirits, speaking in tongues and interpreting tongues. (1 Cor 12:8-11, 1 Cor 12:28)

As you emerge, you need to recognise your spiritual gift and value it, but never at the cost of your flint. Both work together, to bring God glory!

You may be aware of your gift, and for others, you may need to spend some time in prayer and to be taught, in order to understand how each gift functions. This is imperative, because in today's world you need the Holy Spirit's wisdom and guidance, as you learn how to use your gifts in the wider world to bring Him glory!

The world is changing, and there are pressing needs beyond you, time is not allotted for you to sit on your laurels waiting with gifts that are still in foetal stages, because you haven't developed them. Foetal stages? Yes, the gift has barely been unwrapped. Consider for a moment, the times you've heard people say: 'you've got so much potential', 'I see so much more in you'. It sounds flattering to most of you, but it ought to be seen as an invitation for introspection. There's something that they see on the inside of you, that needs to be developed and matured. In order for you to bring greater benefit to world around you, a greater expression of that gift is required.

> *'As every man hath received the gift, even so minister the same **one** to another, as good stewards of the manifold grace of God' (1 Peter 4:10)*

Being a 'good steward' requires accountability on your part. With so much access to resources, why not jump online, read books and broaden your learning from people beyond your immediate culture and setting. What resources are you using to grow your spiritual gift? Have you reached some height that you think you can't push beyond?

Don't neglect the role that your environment plays in the development of your gift. Stimulating environments like the church, times of worship, theological institutions, libraries, small groups, nature walks and prayer, can facilitate growth. Isn't it time to seek atmospheres that help to cultivate the gifts you have, not control, manipulate or use them.

> *The diamonds in your life must be cared for and protected. Its value is high and people will often look to exploit it for selfish gain! Don't be one of those people.*

Be sensitive about where you place yourself, so that you express your gift through the dictates of your Spirit, not the dictates of man. It's from the Spirit, that you can best serve the world beyond you.

I've counselled and prayed for many people who are exhausted, tired and feeling as though they are being used for their gift. Let's cultivate spiritual ethics, and handle others with respect, honour and care. The gifts are not for selfish gain, neither institutional furtherance, but for the proclaiming of the gospel. If you have been affected by this in your life, you have to tell God. Allow, the process of God to re-cut and repair your damaged or broken diamonds. It may mean stepping back from serving in some areas, but that may be exactly what's required as you emerge. Don't fight it, submit to the beautification of God and let the healing virtue flow.

Spend time with God, learn daily about yourself and grow your gifts. It is the Holy Spirit who distributes gifts, so by nature the discovery must be a spiritual experience. Let Him *'teach you all things'* through His word, dreams, visions, the everyday, and through teachers (John 14:26)

Do your part to grow your gift and the gift will bless you.

Your gift has power

'Your gift makes room for you, and brings you before great men' (Prov 18:16)

If you've watched stunning loft conversions, garage conversions or extensions, you understand that the transformation from a space to a room, requires great construction and time. The process of *'making'* is about producing, forming, forging and building. Your gift carries all these remarkable constructive qualities, and as you use your gifts, they will fulfil their purpose.

There are places in life, tables you need to be around, nations you need to travel to, buildings you need to occupy, people you need to meet, and be connected to in this season. You are waiting for them, and they are waiting for you, to mature your gift and use it! Just think on that!

The callings of God in any new season of life, can usher you into new spaces and places. This can lead you into departing from a gift you may have spent years flowing in, to mine another gift, or to use your current gift in a different way. Deep conflicts can arise when you are not conscious of this. This may even be a reason why some of you have been held up and stuck at some point in your life's journey, because you are spending all your time and energy driving activity in one area of gifting, when God is trying to birth something else, in the Spirit. For example, you may have been focusing on teaching when God is directing you to help in the areas of missions, or busy supporting with administration when He's actually leading you to serve in the area of healing, with a children's charity. You may be focused on prophetic singing, when he's actually leading you to teach about fostering healthy relationships through a new blog.

There may be times in your life when you will discover different gifts and be required to use them. Remaining flexible and open to this is key.

Are you finding that you are not flourishing in your gift, the way you used to? Is there a new gift, new method, new strategy or a need for greater growth?

I hope you get this! You are carrying so much more power than you think you are. Power to open doors, power to transform lives, and the power for greater service. *'Be faithful with the little you have and He will make you ruler over much'* (Luke 16:10). Let God unlock your potential as you commit to greater spiritual development. He holds the key. As you trust him with your life, your gifts and talents He's going to lead you to people in the suffering world beyond you, and as you emerge you're going to need a compass to direct you to those who need what you have.

Compassion is the compass

'Gifts are like oil in a car but compassion is what moves you'
Compassion means 'to empathise with someone who is suffering and to feel compelled to reduce the suffering'. (Compassion UK)

Right now, there are a people who are facing injustice, spiritual poverty and physical poverty. You may not know them by name, you may not even be able to define their need, but they are out there. The challenge is that God is trying to get so many of you to move, to respond and to serve those needs. The fact that you are travelling through life, equipped for service, but numb to the suffering beyond you is like living in the world but choosing to not see or hear. It's incredibly easy to become self-consumed and immune to the sufferings of others. You're not moved anymore or touched by the pain, darkness and anguish in the world. Maybe it's because you've seen it all before, the broken families, the theft, the murders, the abused children and the lost identity of an emerging generation. Maybe you're unmoved by the growing number of single mothers and fathers, the suicide and drug rates, but the world is in a critical state and it needs you.

Some of you have been feeling that gut wrenching sense of being lost and not firmly finding your place. You may feel like an emotional wreck at times, but quenching it inside, because something's wrong. You're teaching in the schools, preaching, singing, baking, writing, leading in banking, representing in the courts, but something is missing. Don't ignore that feeling anymore, don't run from that internal discomfort that you feel, as you look around you. Don't avert your eye from what makes you weep, crushes you or breaks you in the world. Don't dismiss those injustices that anger you, that break you. Because at times, beloved, that feeling is the compass of compassion awakening and motivating you, to run towards those who need you.

Pray about it, and get ready to use your talents and gifts, as the Holy Spirit directs you.

I wonder where your compass will you lead you in this season?

My compass led me to South Africa

Poverty has always made me weak and uncomfortable. It arises from a feeling of being powerless, because I don't have the resources, water, food and shelter, to help change the physical depravation and scarcity I see.

In the UK, facts and figures show that there were '*4.2 million children living in poverty in the UK in 2018-19*'. That's around 9 in every classroom of 30 (Child Poverty Action Group). Devastating stats for the Western world. Yet, South Africa, which is where I travelled to in the story below, has extensive poverty. More than 6/10 (62.1%) children aged 0-17, were recorded as multi-dimensionally poor in 2015. (Statistics South Africa) Children are considered to be multi-dimensionally poor, when they are deprived of three out of seven dimensions of poverty (Health, Housing, Nutrition, Protection, Education, Information, Water and Sanitation). The psychological, physical and social development of these children, are detrimentally affected because of this.

I entered South Africa, and it was a seriously hot day. I had travelled out there with a team, as part of a missional trip. The two weeks had us up early, as we travelled with host pastors and outreach teams, to speak to people about the gospel, to pray and to encourage them through their struggles.

On one particular morning, we were told we would be heading to Ashton, a small town in the Western Cape famous for its wines and fruits. We all wore casual clothes, and travelled with expectation. Most of the car journey was filled with the stories and experiences so far in the trip. As we arrived, I looked through the windows of the car at the children running with torn clothes, they were bare foot with dirt in their hair, face and nails. They looked at the team in clean clothes and washed faces, knowing that aside from the team leaders and Pastors, we were foreign to their way of living. We were the strangers on their turf!

The terrain was a light brown mudded land, with small burrows of aluminium looking shacks. In between, there were old bikes, rubbish and old furniture. We all prayed together and then dispatched in pairs of two. As we began walking, we noticed that there were drug addicts that were roaming the area, half conscious, but willing to speak. They informed us that there was a cheap and affordable drug that many in the community were using, that was incredibly dangerous, but had contributed to the many addictions of those living there.

Shack after shack, I looked in awe and with deep conviction at the space in which these 3 or 4 member households were living. How could they all fit in the one room, with a curtain dividing pots and bowls of water, from the plates and mattress on the floor? I couldn't believe people were living like that. However, I was soon distracted by the little smiling faces of the most beautiful children. They seemed to have no care in the world. As I embraced them with hugs, they shared stories of their day, schooling and life. Between the conversations, you couldn't miss the strong smell of urine, and I wondered if these children bathed or even changed their clothes, because they were so stained. The longer I was there, was the more I wanted to understand how they had arrived to be in the situation they were in.

Throughout the day, teenagers, grandmothers, millennials and children, all spoke openly and candidly about their lives. My heart broke as I heard of the extreme hunger and poverty. Some were addicted to drugs, and others had run away from domestic violence situations. As I listened to the first story, it was hard, but story after story was littered with pain. After each conversation we would pray at their request, but it didn't take away the brokenness I felt inside. I wanted to do so much more to take away the pain and the sorrow I saw in their eyes. I realised how privileged I was to have food, drink, warmth, a bed and a home, and It was shamefully humbling. I hid the tears as my heart broke, but I listened to the courage of those families, and their open confessions of poor choices, as I shared the Eternal Hope with them. It was a reminder that there was a life beyond this one, through Jesus Christ. The image of those two days will forever linger in my mind.

Even as I write this, my eyes water!

We sang songs and praised those two days. We watched many men, women, boys and girls choose to follow Jesus. As they learnt of God's unconditional love, some wept, some knelt and many repented.

God used that experience to show me, that at times all you have is the gospel, and there's a broken world waiting for it. Sometimes, you will be enriched with resources to help bring more practical support, but even if you don't, let compassion move you to share the '*the greatest gift of all which is salvation*' (Rom 6:23, Eph 2:8)

Although South Africa was a life changing trip, each season is presenting me with new lessons and challenges, that are sensitising me to the brokenness of others.

Today you need compassion more than ever! And although compassion 'is' something you can teach, it must be produced, because it is a feeling. People can tell you to care, feel empathy or be aware of other's needs, but only when you are moved within, can you be compelled to relieve suffering, bring support or heal the sick (Mark 6:30-44, Luk 9:10-17).

You may be led to do community work in this season, to champion a non-profit that responds to an area of need; to advocate for those who have no voice, or aren't being listened to in an area. You may not be called to those physically poor, but you are called to those poor and broken in spirit, all around you! Wherever compassion is leading, let that be your compass.

Don't over spiritualise other people's problems, when you have been given the practical and spiritual means to bring solutions.

The flint, the diamonds and the compass

As you engage in acts of service, you need to do a heart check. Why are you doing do it? Are you motivated by compassion and love? Or are you serving others, just so that you can be seen? With prayerful consideration, use your gifts and talents as you serve others in the world beyond you. Be open to engaging in intentional compassionate activity, because you will need that compass as you move forward.

As you emerge, let your life inspire and transform others who are trying to find their way. You never know what new opportunities and collaborations will be formed as you do. In talking, sharing and serving others, you will connect with like-minded people, who share the same pull and compassion as you do.

It is widely known that:

> *Partnerships between individuals, 'arise out of compassion, because we become uncomfortable when we see people suffering, and are motivated to reduce suffering to enhance the potential happiness of others'*
> *(The Science and practise of Compassion).*

Be open to the new people you will divinely connect with along this journey. Who knows how those relationships will flourish as you seek to serve God.

I pray that you will mine your flint, discover and use your diamonds, and follow the compass. There are no more excuses and no need for complacency.

The world beyond you is desperate for your service.

The Land Eternal

CHAPTER EIGHT

Strangers

ARE YOU standing behind a closed door curious about the stranger behind it, but not willing to engage or to let them in? Have you been creating your own fences and walls to restrict the access of new people into your life, your groups and networks? Or do you avoid conversation at any cost?

> *Even before the recent Pandemic, many of you were socially distanced from reaching others. You may not have worn visors, masks or carried antibacterial gel, but you had your own bubble. And it was hard for anyone to get in, or to get you out!*

By socially distanced, I am inferring a physical distance and a safe space between yourself and other people.

It's time to ask yourself whether connecting with people is an essential part of your life, or are you doing everything you can to keep people out? Are you doing your best to stay private, undisturbed, and to ignore people as much as possible. If so, it's important to ask yourself: 'why am I like this?'.

I have often heard people say things like, 'I am content with my circle', 'I don't have time', 'I'm happy with the people I have' and 'it's uncomfortable to strike up conversation with someone i don't know'. And as true as all of those responses may be, you are missing the power of your calling to take the message of hope to those who don't know it. In fact, part of your collective identity hinges on the witness of the gospel to the 7.5 billion strangers in the world.

As you emerge, it's important to identify what is actually hindering your ability to reach strangers, to overcome those barriers and to find solutions that facilitate your growth in this area. As you learn to look with a new lens at the world, you need to move beyond the fear of those you are actually called to.

Fear of strangers

The fear associated with new people (strangers), can be birthed out of past experiences. It could be, that when you've dared to invite new people into your lives, or begin a new partnership or conversation, the result was not what you expected. The relationship broke down, people disregarded you, walked away, or said they weren't interested. Your deep hurts of rejection, betrayal and abuse, may still require time to heal. For you, keeping away, keeps you safe, and it's a reasonable conclusion to arrive at. However, if you continue to live life closing people out and hiding from the world, building caves of isolation in order to protect yourself, it will keep you in a place of fear and control, instead of love and trust.

The illusion is, that by isolating yourself from strangers you are somehow keeping yourself safe, so you ignore them and find any excuse not to engage with them, but what you are actually experiencing is an artificial experience created by high levels of fear. As fear rises, you can find yourself running from new relationships, hiding from people who could benefit from your gifts and talents or completely isolating yourself from any social activities that mean engaging with others. What you don't realise, is that when you have a sense of social awkwardness or a reluctance to talk to the new person at work, at church or during social activity, people can often feel it. Your discomfort can begin to cause others to feel uncomfortable, as they sense that their presence is causing you some discomfort and unease. So, be mindful that by approaching strangers from a position of fear, it won't just affect you, but how others perceive you too!

I've known people to leave a room or a conversation, regress into silence, and even be intimidated by strangers they've met! This is all before speaking a word. The challenge is that you can be blinded from seeing an opportunity to connect with people who aren't familiar, instead you may see them as hostile, and that alone can change the way you behave before you've even spoken to them. These patterns of behaviour, diminish how you relate to others that are new, and the effectiveness of your service. Identifying what your past experiences have been, and what you learned, is a good place to start. What happened? What would you do differently?

Don't let your past experiences and your own judgements of strangers constrain you, instead learn to be a little more open and a little less guarded. Let discernment lead.

Not surprisingly, some of your fears of strangers move beyond the shadows of your past experiences.

You see, I genuinely believe that most of you don't view the majority of 'strangers' you pass and meet every day, as representing new opportunities to serve, new collaborations, inspiration or learning. This could be because of the messages most of you gained earlier in your life about strangers.

You grow up in the early part of your life being told 'don't talk to strangers' and to 'be careful of strangers'. This messages comes from your schools, your parents and guardians, it's in the films and the movies you watch, and although there's wisdom in the message, because as children you are often more trusting and sometimes a little less discerning, it produces a context of fear and danger. So, whilst you're being encouraged to go into all the world and transform it, the world is shouting back at you:

> *'don't come this way, the unknown and the strangers are something to be afraid of and out to get you'.*

Because of this, you are defaulted to see most of the people in the world beyond you as dangerous and threatening! The challenge is, that much of what you have learnt as a child is so engrained, that as you reach adulthood, it can be increasingly hard to break free from that way of thinking

Research has shown that our culture prohibits and deters you away from engaging with strangers.

Ellen Kate Donnelly, wrote in an article titled, 'Why you shouldn't be afraid of strangers' that: 'There's a stigma, of imposing ourselves upon others. People we don't know, are kept at arm's length and speaking out is considered weird'.

A BBC report by Nicholas Epley and Juliana Schroeder (behavioural scientists, 2019) agreed, they claim that people spend most of their lives in *'self-imposed isolation every day from*

strangers on their commute, at the park of café because they believe that reaching out will make people uncomfortable'.

Naturally this will have implications on your level of impact and the connections you form throughout your life, because you're not going to open the door with intrigue, to speak to a stranger at work, in the street, at the mall, at the airport or whilst at the bus stop, if you sense your interaction is going to make them or yourself uncomfortable.

As the Holy Spirit began to speak to me in this area, I could perceive many barriers to my own and others emergence. I could see how we have learnt *'to oppress the stranger wrongfully'* through the lens of fear (Ez 22:29) and found ourselves stuck between sharing the truth of the gospel, and a world we're told will reject it. You may have wrestled with the same barriers to reaching people and the same fears, because at times I have. I've avoided conversations because I've felt as though I was interrupting other people's lives or my conversation was inconvenient. However, I have found some solutions and I pray that as you read the next section, that you consider what solutions you are brave enough to begin to incorporate in your own life.

Unless these tensions are exposed and practical solutions given, it will impede on how you reach and serve throughout your life. So, let's reframe how you see strangers.

There is value in strangers

If you want to emerge, you 'have' to perceive and recognise the value of strangers, because just like as the children of Egypt experienced, there are *'strangers that will travel amongst'* you in life (Exodus 12:49). The word *'amongst'* refers to strangers that are central to your life. That means there are people you don't know right now who will play a divine role in your life. I hope you are ready to meet them on the way to work, on the bus, at church, at a social gathering, shopping in Ikea, through social media, whilst on holiday, or in that business meeting.

The bible is littered with examples where individuals connected with strangers. In Luke chapter 5, Peter was having issues on the job when Jesus, who was considered a stranger, came with a solution that helped to provide for him and gave his whole life purpose. There is also the example where Abraham entertained two strangers passing by his tent whom he invited to his house for a meal, in turn they spoke truth to him about the promise of his future and his unborn son. Then there's the two strangers Elijah and Elisha, who met whilst one was passing by and the other was working, the exchange led to Elisha being promoted into Elijah's position as prophet, a role and assignment far greater than tending to oxen. In all these exchanges two or more strangers connected to a divine moment, and their lives were never the same.

In the same way, God has divine connections in mind for you, just as you are going to be the divine connection that someone else is waiting for. It's important to recognise and embrace these relationship gifts He places in your lives. To take the leap to extend the hand, start the conversation and at least make eye contact with the strangers around you.

In an article written by the Guardian, *Stanford professor and renowned sociologist Mark Granovetter writes: 'that while strong ties (family, friends, colleagues) are fundamental to your lives, it's the more distant connections (acquaintances, people you strike up a conversation with at a party, friends of friends,) that are fundamental to your career and holistic development. These connections, provide you with huge opportunities: they are the route in your lives to new projects, new jobs and new ideas'. (Joanna Moorhead 2020)*

The article claims that the very thing we're missing right now, is something we're more in need of than ever, or soon will be are new people. People are jobless, or facing joblessness, people are struggling emotionally and mentally searching for a hope and reason to exist, and its distant connections or strangers who can say: 'have you considered this? Or someone I know might need you to do that, or I can support you here, let me pray for you there'. These individuals who are considered to be those less familiar beyond your circles, all have access to new unique information, experiences and perspectives that you don't hold.

With all that is occurring in our current culture and modern world, this is an opportunity for all to become part of the collective recovery effort. So, *'be not forgetful to entertain strangers...'* (Hebrews 13:2)

Consider the areas where you can focus on improving someone-else's life spiritually, emotionally, financially, educationally or materialistically? Use your flint, diamonds and compass, and let the Spirit lead you to them.

Whatever happens, don't let anything hold you back from new conversations and relationships, not even yourself. When you start talking yourself out of crossing the road to speak to that young girl who is always crying, or from paying for the shopping of that person who was counting pennies in Tesco to pay for their food, remember that this could be an opportunity to connect, relieve someone's suffering and even share the gospel of hope.

Reaching them

I am often observing my environments when I am shopping, at work and just taking a stroll at the park. I am not necessarily seeking connection, but I am trying to be aware and discerning.

During my emergence I awoke to the deep value of strangers again, and I was intentional about connecting and conversing with those I met on my daily travels. I began striking up a conversation in the carpark with fellow drivers about little things, like the lack of parking, connecting with the person who agreed the weather just constantly rains, greeting the DPD delivery guy after each delivery, and striking conversations with the cashiers at the tills during my shop. At times people would ask me if I knew these individuals because of the striking familiarity of tone in my approach, and I would reply no. But what I was exercising was the new confidence and liberty I felt to speak to strangers. What I was learning was that I had to take the first step, and more than often I was received well. As I continued to do this I formed new friendships, bonded with people who are called to areas of work similar to my own, shared the gospel, and connected with people who have been a tremendous support to me. Beyond the practical benefits of reaching strangers, I have realised just how easy it is to begin conversations, and to open the doors to knowing others.

Sometimes I think some of my confidence to talk to random people came from my old roles as a recruitment consultant where you have to pick up the phone and speak to strangers asking them what their needs are for staffing, and trying to fill their roles. Overcoming the fear of picking up the phone to make my first call was a huge task, but as I learnt on my first day:

The other person is human, they have needs like you do, remember that you're trying to help them find a solution.

As you live with this perspective, you can remove some of the unnecessary pressure you put on yourself and enjoy the path.

One thing that I have loved is the beauty of personalising my transactions with others. Sometimes it was through the token smile, helpfulness, asking for their name or calling them 'my lovely'. Simple interactions made such a difference, like a 'hello' or the acknowledgement of 'Juan' in the coffee shop at the train station (Juan is just a name that came to me because I keep forgetting his real name!). Don't underestimate the power of making eye-contact and having genuine conversations with others, it's a good place to start. So many people are craving meaningful conversations to share their views, values, interests and experiences. Respond to them by showing your humanity - that you care. You'll soon realise that one moment can change everything, as you invite others to be open.

In addition, creating an economy of exchange is powerful.

There are opportunities that you will have to collide with others, and sometimes through that connection there are unexpected interests that arrive. You may not satisfy those interests, you may not the be right person for the job, you may not have the money to help them, you may not be right person for the organisation, or the right person to advocate on their behalf. You may not be the right person to create a solution in that area, or to serve in that area of ministry. For this reason, you may shy away, but instead create an economy of exchange, and look at your connections, is there someone you know that could provide the answers to those interests? The friend, the colleague, the strangers you met last week, or the family member could all be helpful solutions.

It's easy to live with a satisfy myself mentality, but be your brother's keeper. Look for ways in which you can masterfully play your part, because you will achieve greater things together than you will ever do on your own.

> *'Let the ethos of your life be to bring
> greater value to the lives of those around you
> and greater transformation'*

At times, your level of exchange will actually require you making a financial investment in someone-else's journey. To put your hands in your pocket, to tap that card, make that cash app or PayPal payment into someone-else's account to support them. You may not think it's a significant amount, but sow a seed into the soil of their land. Because:

> *'your seed speaks'*

I never saw it before, but I have learnt that at times when I was lead to sow a few hundred pounds into new businesses, or other people's lives, that they always came back to tell me what it meant to them. For some the financial seed let that person know that I care, for another lady it showed her to keep believing and to keep on going.

You could be paying for someone's shopping or their petrol, leaving an envelope for a struggling colleague in their pigeon hole, blessing a struggling family with money to buy clothes for their children, placing some money in the hand of someone homeless or giving to a charity. And it may not be a whole amount to you, but you are helping them to yield a far greater harvest in the future by making that investment. You may make a cash investment that increases someone else's faith, hope and belief that there's a God who sees, cares and knows. Don't feel compelled to give, but choose *'not to withhold good from those to who it is due, when it is in your power to do it* (Prov 3:27) No matter how little or how much you have, the generous will be blessed (Prov 22:9)

Don't be stingy and don't hold back during your emergence. Don't do it for recognition, or to seek a reward, because if you do you are not connecting with others from a pure place, but from a place of revenue. You want to get something back out of it.

> *'Let each of you look out not only for his own interest, but also for the interests of others' (Phi 2:4)*

There are many strangers in the world beyond you that you will meet, but some are more significant than others. Navigating according to the Spirit's leading is key. At times it can be hard to discern those new connections as you adjust to God's leading and direction.

The strangers you need to see

The world is a room and you must read it correctly in each new season. Change is here!

During my emergence, I found myself in many new contexts with new meetings and new conferences. I had new people referring me to do work, and great opportunities to serve people.

My initial feeling was fear, because so many of these people were new (strangers). Out of my own anxiety, I became ultra-protective about who I allowed into my life. I kept getting messages from young women asking me to mentor them, asking for advice, asking to be part of future programmes. My response was, 'no, no, no'. I also had specific people who began giving money for my future projects and work, none of which I had discussed with them. And my initial response was, I'm not sure of your motives, so 'no, no, no'. It all happened quickly, and it was very overwhelming, so I said, no, no and no to new connections, new people and some opportunities.

The problem was, that I couldn't discern that I was in a new land, a different place, and the path up ahead was filled with many strangers.

As you step into new and familiar contexts, you must be careful that you are interpreting your new environments and people correctly. This is because anything new, is initially hard to process, due to your lens bias.

Your lens is processing life from information, but the new lens takes time to adjust. The lens is about how you see the world beyond you and your process of selection. Everyone engages in selection every day, subconsciously, as you choose what and who you will attend to, and those you will dismiss. From events and conversations, to people you perceive, your mind is filtering the world beyond you. This is based heavily on information that you hold about yourself, the world around you and your calling. The problem is, that most of you have been governing your lives by old information for so long, that it blocks and ignores anything new. For example, in this season of your life, many of you have focused on particular types of people, with particular abilities. You've entered into particular types of relationships, and focused on those from particular backgrounds and cultures, more than others. They may be male, female, black, white or Asian, middle-aged, young or old. The bias operates by drawing your focus to the same people, and neglects others. This is great if God is calling you to focus on a particular group, but it also restrains you if the new information that God shows, is leading you towards another group or people.

I am passionate about this, because there are many writers, including the more popular Malcolm Gladwell, author of *'Talking to Strangers'*, who agree that there is something fundamentally wrong, with how we all understand people different from ourselves. He claims that people read others at work, in their communities, and at social events, based on looks, body language, character and opinions. That what you initially perceive about a person, is based on how you interpret the data you are receiving through your physical senses rather than the spirit. And that bias will exclude some people and include those you have a natural preference towards.

Let's look at a biblical example of this.

Samuel a man of God, nearly chose to appoint a man called Abinadab, a son of Jesse, to a highly esteemed position of king, but the instruction from God was: *'Look not on his countenance, or on the height of his stature; because I have refused him: for the LORD seeth not as man seeth, for man looks on the outward appearance but God looks at the heart'* (1 Sam 16:7)

As Samuel listened to God he was drawn away from the outward appearance. He asked Jesse if he had any other sons and Jesse redirected him towards a young, grubby man who was a shepherd boy. His name was David, and he was chosen and anointed to become the king of Israel.

If Samuel had trusted his own bias, he would have chosen the wrong man, but he remained open to the Holy Spirit and made an important selection.

As you push forward in the journey, you will need to adopt a new strategy because the old simply won't work. Your natural instinct will be to serve, to have a conversation, or to say 'yes and no', to all the people you did before, but next time take a long pause before you respond. Consider what the moment is presenting. Stay listening to God, and be led by the Holy Spirit your teacher who will help you perceive the world more accurately. At times you will have to go the extra mile to make a conscious effort as you build the relationships that you sense God is forming. If he's calling you to a particular group, area or location, then do the research and take the time to be more informed and educated about people you don't know – people of a different race, culture, age, class or religion. You can't afford to miss connections, networks, people and opportunities, because of your lens bias.

The Call to Strangers

Some of you are being called to a new set of people (strangers) to serve them, I hope you are open to that!

I recall a time when one of my brothers came to hear me preach at a large church in London, and he spoke to me at the end of the service. He said, 'Sharlette, it's not this, there's so much more. Do you know how many people out there, men and women, would listen to you?'. I was taken back. But his words were like water to my Spirit. It was the raw truth I needed to hear! It was a wakeup call. It resonated with me, because my ability to see people beyond the ones I already engaged with, or beyond the ones who were familiar, was faint.

God was using my brother to change my mind through introducing new information and revelation, that I needed to hear. This was fundamental to the next part of my journey, although what he said was hard to hear. What my brother didn't know, was that I had several dreams months before of women being trafficked and children being physically abused.

A few months after his comments, I began having dreams about women who needed to be liberated from trafficking and needed to be empowered. My initial thought was 'no, God couldn't be calling me into this'. I have no lengthy experience, neither have I studied in this area. But, God doesn't need any of that to call you. He just needs you to yield, to trust and obey. As I have done just that, I've seen the hand of God teach, train and equip me to serve these women day by day.

Some of you are already doing tremendous good as you reach strangers though different activities, but I wonder if God is encouraging you to reach a new group of strangers? Does He keep sending the same message through different people, to call you in a new direction? Or maybe He's asking you to serve those you already do, better.

Understanding those He's calling you to in this time is key. Is it children, men, women, divorced, impoverished, business people or political people?

Going with God, can seem foolish to the wise and be an isolating and lonely experience. No-one can believe for you in these seasons. It's all on you, and it will require a level of faith and risk to trust His leading and to follow. Some people will never understand the sacrifices God asks you to make, but you have to find peace with that! The fact is, that sometimes where God's calling you, and the strangers He's asking you to reach and serve, are way beyond your current accomplishments, abilities and experience. Because:

You're not always moving you into a place of interest

For years, some of you have been taught that you will reach those who share parts of your life's story. I was taught this too, for many years. You have been told, that you have gone through some tests in life, that will connect you with another person's story, and inspire them through your own survival. And although that is true in part, the bible is flooded with people who went through nothing remotely similar to the people that they were sent to.

Jonah from Gath-hepher, was commissioned to travel to Nineveh, and though reluctant and running in the opposite direction for part of it, he fulfilled his mission (Jonah 1) He had nothing in common with their culture, and wasn't even from amongst their people. Look at Phillip, he was an administrator who was attending to temporal affairs in Jerusalem, and supporting the Apostles. He felt compelled by an inward call, to run as an evangelist towards Samaria and preach the gospel. As he preached, he saw signs and wonders with miraculous healings (Acts 8). Then there's Moses, he was called to be a leader for the children of Israel. Yes, he was Hebrew, but he didn't grow up amongst them. He had no experience of what it was like to be a Jewish man suffering under the oppressive system, and brutality of Egypt. Yet he was called to reach them and lead them (Ex 3)

'You won't always feel a sense of belonging to those you are connected with'

And that may be hard hitting in a culture that promotes a sense of 'belonging'. You can connect through the call and compassion to act and do, but you don't need to belong, to fit in. If you walk through life expecting to be drawn to those you have commonalities with or feel a member of, you will be limiting your reach.

I believe this has already crippled so many in their understanding and direction of calling.

You must never confuse your passion and experience with your calling. You may have no experience with some of the people you are called to reach in this season. They may seem alien to you. Nothing like you, different races, classes, cultures and histories, and yet you are called to them.

Don't get nervous, you can do this!

It's time to weigh up the information you hold about the calling on your life, and the strangers you are sent to. The world is in crisis and you are part of Gods solution. Decide the pathway you will pursue.

Unlock the path

The path awaits, look ahead.

In the famous story found in the book of Ruth, two women were given the same choice to travel to Bethlehem (a new land, a different language and filled with strangers) or return back to Moab (Home, familiar land and people). Both women were broken at the loss of their husbands, and had the right to depart from their mother in law. She even encouraged them to go back to Moab; that life prospects were better there.

'But, in a world of Orpahs, who turn away from the chance to venture into the unknown and go back to the familiar, be a Ruth.

Ruth heard the call, and refused to go back, she was ready for the unknown, fuelled with optimism and hope. I imagine Ruth was packing her bags, mumbling to herself 'you don't have to tell me twice, I need a new start, I need a new life, and I refuse to stay here. I'd prefer to dwell amongst the strangers than to remain in the safety of my own comfort. *'Where you go, I will go...Your people shall be my people...'* (Ruth 1:16-17)

It's time for some of you to stop toying with the idea of going where God's calling you, and believe what He has said concerning your life. Run towards the world with the message of hope and truth. Share the gospel with strangers, and cease the opportunities merited through these times of social, political and economic unrest.

Now is the time to go! Because if you don't run towards your calling, beyond your comfort. If you don't heed the call that beckons you forward, you will pay for it. You will get down life's road and lament over the life you missed out on. You will mull over the should haves, could haves and would haves. And you will regret the opportunities that were squandered because of fear and anxiety of the world beyond you.

The new strangers that are up ahead, may be some of the most incredible or challenging people you have ever met. You might be led to reach an unreached people group. It may be the challenge of moving into a new industry, building an establishment on new land, engaging vulnerable individuals from prostitution, or supporting the homeless. It may be starting a new business, or launching a ministry that responds to the pressing needs of a community. Maybe it's reaching strangers who have language barriers and other personal obstacles that may not allow them free access to hearing the gospel. It could be extending the climb towards those in poverty stricken countries with limited resources, or extending the arm towards the strangers you meet every day.

No matter where it is or who they are, risk the rejection, take the opportunity and run with faith as you reach people along life's path.

CHAPTER NINE

Extraction

'As you emerge, spend your wealth and all its power, in the richest lands of human spirit and soul.'

LIFE IS full of extractions, they are the moments when others can draw something out, or pull something from your life. It's also when you can draw something from others' lives too.

Sometimes what we pull from people's lives can bring positive value to our own, and at other times it can be negative and harmful. However, each experience can bring great significance in this natural course of giving and taking, because there are always lessons to be learnt. It's all part of the great exchange in life.

Extraction

The scripture from 2 Corinthians 9:6-8 reminds us of the value of these exchanges:

> *'Remember this: Whoever sows sparingly will also reap sparingly, and whoever sows generously will also reap generously'*

The culture of sowing, defined through acts of giving are not just about making monetary deposits, which is where this verse is commonly used, but it's about giving out of the abundance that you have received. This could be in the form of giving your time, energy, gifts, talents, prayer and the ways you share the gift of salvation.

I say this passionately, because during my emergence, I realised that I was intentional about giving in many of the areas mentioned above, but I had lost my responsibility to share the gospel with those who didn't know it. Nearly 70% of my time was spent being a light amongst other lights, even though I was called to *'shine my light in the darkness'* (John 1:5). But God convicted me, that in times such as these, with economic, moral, social and political unrest, there must be a greater attempt to reach humanity. From the depths of my compassion, I should be driven to transform others with the message of hope.

Some of you may feel the same, as that tension to run towards the darkness arises. You may be giving of your time in fulfilling good deeds through social impact and compassionate activity, which all has its place, but unfortunately, that's not enough. And yes, there are many articles, research and findings that support the need for a mutual overlapping of both social and spiritual impact in our communities, but in my view, one should never be at the cost of the other. The starving person that is hungry needs food for the body, but they also need food for the spirit too.

I am no stranger to the demands and sacrifices that have to be made as you put the needs of others above your own. Sometimes it's easier said than done, and it goes against the popular message, 'do you'. However, as you emerge you have to be led by the spirit, with an eternal consciousness to reach others.

Extracting the Eternal Consciousness

At times, I was lost in a fury of activity, running my business, spending time with family, travelling to beautiful locations and flying out for ministry invitations, but I had lost my perspective of an eternal consciousness. I knew I had an eternal destiny, but very few times would I really think about it. This was because I rarely heard messages about life eternal preached, and secondly because I didn't think much about Heaven. I was family conscious, self-conscious, financially conscious and politically conscious, but eternal...no!

Most of you may live this way, with a disconnect around the eternal life beyond this one. However, it's essential to keep the bigger picture in mind.

John S Dunne writes:

> *'It is the life of the spirit that is the eternal in us, the inner life of knowing...if there were no eternal consciousness in a man, what then would life be but despair?'*

As God began to speak to me about this, it was as if my spirit was connecting again to the Eternal land beyond. I knew that even in my own life, I was despairing about many things that over time began to lose their importance.

I wonder if your loss of the eternal consciousness, is altering your perspective of life? Could that be why some of you are despairing and getting caught in anxieties and fears about your future?

I know it's not easy amidst a world fuelled by distractions, but it is paramount to bring that the eternal is kept in view as you emerge. There ought to be something in you that pulls you beyond your comfort zones and draws you to save souls.

It's time to extract the life transforming power of the spirit within again, and to recognise what else may be hindering the flow.

Sometimes, God has to pull the power out of you

You have an infinite, unlimited and eternal power living on the inside of you, it's time you lived like it!

At times it's easy to forget. You can lose the sense of the eternal value you bring to the world, and the responsibility to change it. But, within you is the power to transform the lives of others and to change the way they live. This power comes through the Holy Spirit, but you've got to use it. It's not arriving from somewhere beyond you, from people or environments, no it's flowing from the well within; *'the fountain of life.'* (Psalms 26:9) It's just waiting to be realised and released into the lives of others.

Consider this:

As Brian sat at the table of life asking for water. The waiter came and said there Is already water in your cup and walked away. Brian tipped the cup upside down and saw nothing, he calls the waiter the second time and says 'I'd like some water'. As the waiter walks to the table, he brings a second glass and tips the first glass into the second. He lifts the glass showing Brian the water. 'How?' said Brian. The waiter replied: 'In life, you will only recognise the power of what you have as you pour it out'.

The challenge is that if you don't know how to use the power given to you, and how to dispense it, you will use it incorrectly, or completely disregard it. This has led some of you to use the power of the Spirit as a means to influence others. But the power of the Spirit has been given to do more than influence those around you.

Any man or woman can influence: the businessman, the makeup artist, the politician, the shop keeper, drug dealer and school teacher, all influence those around them. It is simply, *'the capacity to change or affect someone or something: the power to cause changes without directly forcing them to happen.'* (Merriam Webster)

You only have to look at the modern world, and you can see how saturated our culture has become with Influencers, they are everywhere. Online they are presenting people with ideas, food, concepts, new ways of thinking, motivation, places, and inspiration that people may not have regularly found. Woven in-between, are those who try to inspire your life with talks and seminars, and they are all vying for your attention, to keep you more positive or optimistic about the prospects of your life. Each selling their own values, morals, perspectives and outlooks. All you need is a good story, a good presenting style and to connect with your audience.

The challenge is, that you aren't called to influence, instead you are called to bring inner transformation, because that's what Jesus did. He went out transforming communities where people extracted his teachings, truth and an eternal world view (Mark

10;1, Mark 9:3 Matt7:9). Through His death, we extracted life, and through His spirit we are encouraged to share this message with all those who cross our path. This transformation brings a new heart and a whole new Spirit *(Ezek. 36:26-27)*, and its mandatory in order to discover Gods plan. So as you come alongside those you are called to reach, and as you cross the paths of the stranger, know that you have the power to transform lives.

Power can be extracted from your life as you challenge and change the beliefs of others. As you serve your communities, work at your job, and as you travel through life - look for opportunities to share the gospel. Pray for others and use your words to speak life, because you have the power to bring change in the places you cannot go, and amongst the people you cannot see. The beauty of prayer is that it doesn't have to infringe anyone, you can pray wherever you are, at home, in the kitchen, the bathroom at work or whilst walking, and no-one can stop you from praying. It's your right and one of the great privileges and powers you have in your arsenal. And when you don't know what to pray *'the Spirit himself will intercede'* (Romans 8:26) No matter where you are in life, unleash the transformative power of your prayer.

As you stand in the light of your callings, let your humility of character and compassionate conduct lead the way. Let others see something different about the way you are living your life, that causes people to be attentive to what you do. Are you serving with patience, exhibiting love, reaching with compassion or easily forgiving? These are just some of the attractive qualities that often welcome people into our lives. As they enquire, let people come into the truth, that there is a life beyond this one, and a God who sent His son to die for them. Remind them that they too can be grafted into an eternal plan for salvation, intentionally playing their part. This is what makes your service so powerful. You get to show people through your life and conduct, that there is a better system of living, led by the Spirit.

It's time to stop holding back, because people need you. Let God lead you to bring robust change and a new perspective of life, to those in your workplace, homes, communities and institutions. That is the power you yield. It's time to let others extract it!

Sometimes extractions are being made and you are not even aware

What makes extractions so amazing is that most times it's happening and you're not even conscious of it. There are connections and activities taking place every day of our lives, and many people are being transformed at unexpected times.

Sometimes people are being transformed through your presence, words and activities but they will never tell you.

I worked with a very talented young girl. I had taught her for a few years and I loved teaching her. Every visit, her mother and sister would use the time to share the week's activities and update me on 'all things family'. That's right, I got a comprehensive breakdown, but all I would do was listen as they fought for space to speak between the overlapping conversations. In between, I'd offer some advice. I only travelled to teach there 1 hour a week, but I enjoyed their company, and they became family to me. I was about to commence the session, when the child's mother stopped me and said, '*I want to share something with you, I've been meaning to say this since last week*'. She said:

'There's something different about you, I can't quite put it into words. But each time that I hear your voice, even in my home, the atmosphere changes and sometimes I get goose bumps. You inspire us, and I hope that you can be in the lives of my children through to their adulthood, because I want them to know you'.

I had no words, it took me completely off guard. This was mainly because I spent so little time with them and between advice, I had probably prayed once for them upon request. This was the second parent who was experiencing the manifested presence of the Holy Spirit. The first was the mother of a boy that I taught, but it was a bit different.

I had said my goodbyes and I was already five minutes late before my next tuition appointment. They lived in a block of high rise flats, so I had to wait for the lift to come in order to get to the carpark. I was knocking my car keys against my leg anxiously because I was late, and then the lift arrived. 'Finally' I thought. As the doors opened, I heard the Holy Spirit say, 'give her back the £20.00 she gave you for tuition, and walk back to the house and pray for the mother'. My face froze. The lift doors were open, I was already late and God was asking me to turn back and pray for the mother of one of my pupils. So we had a quiet exchange in the silence. Anyone walking by would have seen me standing and starring into the lift with jazz music playing, but inside there was a whole exchange of rock 'n' roll.

I went back and knocked the door, as I did the child's mother answered and said, 'I just knew you'd come back', I was humbly unamused. I placed the money gently in her hand and began to pray for her. As I did a heavy downpour of rain began. She was crying and weeping, and her son stood there looking at me with shocked eyes and the expression: 'Miss Reid is that you?'. After the prayer I hugged her and I left. Now I was nearly 15 minutes late for my next appointment. I had to call and apologise, then trudge through the rain to my car.

It's one thing when you pray for transformation in an area and you see it, such as I have. On multiple occasions I've witnessed the

Holy Spirit heal diseases, disabilities, save people and deliver them, however, it's different when the spirit is working beyond you in least likely settings.

Although, I had connections with these families through teaching, I had no idea that transformation was happening in a significant way. Something about both of those moments broke me on the inside, because I marvelled at the incredible nature of the Holy Spirit, to move in the everyday work activities and settings I usually take for granted. It was clear, that somewhere in the stillness, deep and transformative power was being released through the spirit.

Although I was made aware of these extractions, there are people who will extract healing, hope, inspiration, positivity and other changes without ever telling you.

Some will extract and go

The bible talks about the woman with the issue of blood, recorded in Luke 8: 43-48. She had been to every doctor around town, and none could treat her infirmity of bleeding. But the scripture records that she went to Jesus, behind him, and touched the border of his garment, and immediately her issue of blood stopped. Interestingly, she stood in a place where she couldn't be seen and reached for a part of his garment, making an extraction of healing before she went. What's strange is that she had no intention of telling anyone that she had been immediately healed.

Whether it was out of shame, guilt or for some other reason, this woman extracted healing virtue and then tried to hide.

As you speak to the woman at work who confides in you, or as you help the man who struggles to pay for his shopping; even as you prayed with your manager who shared he's going through divorce, neither may come back to tell you how you impacted their lives. But, you mustn't get lost in the desire to know.

Transformation is being extracted from your spirit, whilst you are in your homes, workplaces, areas you've travelled, and places you've socialised. But maybe you've been diminishing your transformative power, because you don't have a catalogue of all the names of people and places you've brought change? At the end of the day, God is not keeping a tally chart of how many extractions were made from your life, because it's not a competition. We don't all need to know how many people were healed on Wednesday, how many people received your prophecy, how many thousands were saved at your outreach, but should God make you aware, let your boast be in Him as He shows off His attributes. (1 Cor 1:13)

The truth is, that there are many extractions happening in the realm of the Spirit, the intentional ones and the ones you are not aware of. It's not imperative for you to know all the workings of the spirit, but it's important to know that He's working beyond you. Just play your part.

Extracting truth - The Eternal Movement

'As you live in the truth of your spiritual nature you can cross into greater liberty for more extractions'

Somewhere in life's journey, I had embraced a teaching that's quite commonly sold. It states that God can only move on the earth through man, and that somehow God was confined through this. But it's a lie, and it really hindered my growth as it created a block in my spiritual life. God had to remind me that by virtue of his omnipresence (omni) all, and presence (present) God is everywhere at all times, with no exceptions. In fact, for those still playing hide and seek with God, Psalms 139:7-10 details there's no where you can go from the presence of God, *'no where you can flee'*. He has been in the world from the beginning and will continue to be here, way after each person have gone. Hence, He is known as the 'Alpha and the Omega' 'the beginning and the end' (Rev 21:6; Rev 22:13). His spirit was witnessing to people throughout the old testament such as Abraham (Gen 17 - called to be the father of nations), Moses (Ex 3 – God speaks to Moses from the burning bush), Jacob (Gen 28:10-22- Jacob's first encounter as God sends him home) in each example, the Spirit of God transformed their lives without man present. By the New Testament, Acts 9 records Paul encountering Jesus Himself on the Damascus Road as the voice is heard saying: 'Saul, Saul why do you persecute me'. (Acts 9:4-5)

These examples demonstrate that the Spirit of God is not idly waiting to do everything through man, He is working beyond man. When you understand that God is working through you and beyond you in the world, it gives you a very different perspective of life.

The analogy God showed me, was this:

> *'Imagine that you have been given a part as a new cast member in a major production, but millions have played their own parts before you. When you arrive in the theatre, the staging is already there, and there is an existing team of people who are placed to work with you in the production. As you learn to understand your role, you will still have to take instructions and cues from the Director.*
>
> *The play isn't starting because you turned up, and your role is no more significant than those that came before you, or will come after you. However, you are connecting to an*

existing production, and you're learning to do your part'

I love the image of playing my part in the incredible architecture of Gods eternal plan – to understand where my own boundaries and limitations are. It was so refreshing to walk in truth, because that revelation alone, reframed my understanding of the Spirit.

Who knows, maybe Shakespeare was onto something when he said:

'All the worlds a stage, and all the men and women merely characters: they have their exits and their entrances; and one man plays many parts...' (Shakespeare)

Now more than ever you must learn to sharpen your ability to discern the truth from what's false, to align with God's expectations for your lives, and to detach from the fantasies you hold about yourself.

This leads me to the last area of extraction that was key during my emergence.

Extracting your authentic spiritual-self

As part of my transition, God took me on a journey. For several months, He led me to look at some of the historical figures in the Christian faith. I focused on the people that brought great transformation to the lives they touched. I learnt about the life of Kathryn Kuhlman, born in 1907 who was arguably one of the most influential figures, as she changed a generation's understanding of healing and crusade evangelism. She heeded the call and dedicated her life to it, despite the negative press and criticism. Then I looked at the compassion that Mother Teresa born 1910, taught, as she heeded the call in her lifelong commitment to India's poor and neglected. Then there was Dr Martin Luther King, born 1929, the Christian minister and activist, who heeded the call and underpinned the mass movement of equal rights, inspiring a whole generation to rethink racial equality and justice in the United States. In times of hardship, each one defined their lives with bravery, strength and courage as they served, paving a way for others to come thereafter. I could go on, from Evans Roberts (1904-1905), who led the Welsh revival, William Branham (1909-1965) the faith healer who led a revival post-war, Smith Wigglesworth (1859-1947), the apostle of faith as he was known, who led a healing ministry, and lastly William Seymour (1870-1922) the holiness preacher who initiated the Azusa Street revival. They all had a remarkable quality, they trusted the Holy Spirit, and *'though they didn't always know where they were going, they always knew who they were with'* (David Platt).

The lessons I learnt from history showed me time and time again, that each one broke from the ranks of safety and risked it all. They stepped into the middle of the road undaunted, with the traffic of life moving. Something was pulling them forward, a deep inner call, a knocking that compelled them to see a vision of the world that was greater than the one they lived. As they did, they halted others in their path causing them to stop and question, to stare, to oppose and to marvel. They risked it all to see people, places, communities and nations transformed. What an incredible example.

They all had the courage to keep going when they were called rebels, trouble-makers or defiant. I saw courage when they were imprisoned, went through divorce, were tarnished and shamed. In fact, life's tests and the criticism that came with it, did not rob them of their vision and calling, instead it furnished them with an unstoppable determination to keep on going.

You see the more that I learnt about them, was the more that I was feeling convicted. It was not birthed from the need to be like them, but by their outright fearless commitment. I realised that in my walk, I had lost that deep inner tug, that authentic rhythm to my life. I used to have an excitement, an unpredictability and a sense of adventure and trust in the Holy Spirit. However, somewhere beyond the mountain of trials and the valley of decisions, I had become fearful. I was afraid to be different, to stand out to the world unashamed. I asked myself 'what changed'? time and time again, 'when did the shift happen'? 'Where was the radical woman I once knew?' although I asked myself, I knew the answer.

I reflected on the years when I would show myself, my strangeness, quirkiness, and authenticity and it would come out with a mild humour. At times when I would speak, the Holy Spirit would take over, no need for notes, pens or tablets at the time. But it didn't take long before people called me 'radical', 'unusual', 'rebellious' and 'different'. In my early days, I was opposed and made to feel as though I didn't fit into the status quo, and oftentimes I would look around and think the same. 'Why, can't you just fit in!'.

As these old thoughts rose to the surface, so did the feelings, and I realised that those words had left a stain on my identity. I lived for many years with deep insecurities that I didn't quite fit in anywhere. But the Holy Spirit wanted me to come to terms with this. He didn't care what anyone else thought, He just wanted me to know that flaws and all, I was loved by Him (1 John 4:19). As God daily reaffirmed His love towards me, the residue of the past was being healed. I had come to terms with the truth that:

The more I knew I was loved by God, was the more I began to see and embrace my uniqueness in a real and unashamed way. I found peace with all my nuances, my seriousness, comical side and very quirky childish side too.

I remember travelling to America for a speaking engagement in New York in 2019, and the Lord really moved in that place. As I left I began hearing, 'you're unconventional', 'you're unusual', 'there's something different about you', and ordinarily I would've clammed up inside and seen it as though something was wrong with me, but I knew I had changed, because I simply said 'thankyou'.

It took years for me to embrace my weird patterns and ways, but I thank God I'm not afraid anymore. *'I'm fearfully and wonderfully made'* (Psalms 139:14). Now I embrace what makes me different, as part of the unique flavours and fragrance that I bring to life! I'm free to be me, and to encourage others to do the same, and it's one of the greatest areas of my emergence.

The ability to first recognise what makes you different, is a key part to understanding who you are.

> *'When you are clear about what makes you a unique individual, you can give to others. You can know your unique place in the world and the purpose God has for you'*
> *(Viktor Kubik 2013)*

You are unique, and some of you need to embrace your peculiarities rather than reject them or you use them to disqualify yourself. Rather than supress who you are, learn to see the beauty in what you bring and what you do. As you serve you have to recognise that God wants to use the whole you, not the bits and pieces you offer after you've belittled or talked yourself down.

A great way of celebrating and recognising your inner beauty, is to explore some of your own innate qualities which are often overlooked, and under celebrated. Maybe you're smart, funny, courageous, empathetic, resilient, sensitive, dynamic, well-humoured, charismatic, serious or intense, to name a few. Take the time to write some of these qualities down, and then thank God for them. 'Why?' You may ask. Well, some of these qualities are precisely why 'you' have been uniquely chosen to carry out particular future tasks or assignments. With a little work, those attributes could become a masterful asset in the role that God wants you to play. I have often found that, we don't always invest in innate qualities because we take innate character qualities for granted. Yet, those qualities are what makes you distinguishable, so always pay attention to what makes you different in a world marred by the desire for sameness.

Are you missing the opportunity to inspire others with what makes you different, fragrant, colourful and attractive? To step out as you, all of you, your authentic self?! God can work with and work on that. God doesn't want a perfect person He wants a willing person who surrenders all of who they are to His Godly assignments. You must be willing to ask yourself the hard questions, like am I really being true to myself? Don't hide away in the shadows. The Spirit in you is yearning to live freely through your courage, boldness and peculiarities to transform the world beyond. Bring it all!

As you can extract from the Holy Spirit, the Holy Spirit will extract from you, to bless, empower and transform the world. Staying connected to the Eternal consciousness will help you live with perspective. As you do, recognise that you are connecting to an existing movement to save humanity, and you are just learning to play your role with the time you have been given.

Don't be affronted with what makes you different, instead learn to embrace it.

CHAPTER TEN

Critics

'You will never experience real liberty, as long as you are bound by the limited views and opinions of others'.

AS YOU pursue your callings, reaching those you are called to serve, you won't be left to swan through life untouched by criticism. In fact, just as you step out to do something new, the criticism can become increasingly loud.

There are some people who will feel threatened by your new strength and presence. That, combined with a greater use of your gifs and talents, discernment, confidence and character, can all be a bit intimidating for some. You will have to get used to that! It's all part of breaking into the new, it ought to feel different, and a bit uncomfortable. But, don't be phased by this. Don't be fearful of the faces and opinions of others.

In my own life, I have learnt that the negative comments, unfollows, gossips, slandering, rejection and dislikes, are all part of life. Learning to be conscious of this fact, allows you to see all things as working together for the good, rather than to see it as something that is in conflict with the good. It's not personal criticism, it's woven into the fabric of life.

As you mature in your emergence, you will begin to see how each season is forming a rich environment for inner growth and endurance. Criticism can bring unease and pain at times, but it's working as part of your greater purpose.

The challenge is, that some of you have been avoiding criticism all your life, which has bridled your potential for years! Just the thought of how others will respond to your life choices has crippled you, as you live a life of compromise, too afraid to do anything that could offend! However, in the end it will only hurt you, because you are diminishing your own value. The eagerness to please others has led some of you to live with a façade, because you are not being genuine in the expression of who you are, you change the way you talk, change your views and the things you do, all to impress other people. But, it's time to stop living under the thumb of other people's approval or disapproval.

The scripture says:

> 'The fear of man brings a snare, but whosoever trusts in the Lord shall be safe'.
> (Proverbs 29:25)

Don't fall into the trappings that have you living in fear. This is the time to push beyond the views of your friends, family, colleagues and strangers as you push into a place of safety and freedom. There you will find that the presence of God is greater than the oppression of other people's views.

The time is now for you to champion the way forward, whether people like it or not! As you advance with boldness, there are some fundamental lessons that I am going to share, that will help you survive your inner and external critics.

Lesson one: It's you

> *The pervasive worldview, is that those beyond you are your most dangerous critics, but actually your greatest foe is the critic within. This limited understanding, is part of the obsessive attachment in this generation to what is beyond, rather than what is within!*

If you haven't already, you will soon realise that change draws out your inner critical voice much greater than before. As you venture into the unknown, that voice can speak in an attempt to damage your confidence to progress. You may hear phrases like: 'don't do it', 'you weren't made for this', 'you will fail'. And what's frightening is that it's speaking in your voice!

So much of the time, what is standing between you and a higher level of service....is you. That's not to say there aren't other challenges beyond you, but more often than not your inner critic can be more vicious than most of the other external critical voices. Hence, you can be your own worst enemy!

During my emergence, the inner critical voice became aggressively louder. It embarked on a personal onslaught to generously devalue me. It shouted at me with force, 'you shall not pass', like the demon on the bridge, from Lord of the Rings, in an effort to sway my decisions, and get me to retreat from work I knew

I had to do. It has tried to undermine my sense of self-esteem, confidence, and my ability to pursue efforts in my ministry and broader life. If you think that's bad, the inner critic has demonstrated its power to talk whilst other people are talking, and it can be incredibly rude! I've known people to be mid-way through a strong conversation of encouragement, only for the 'inner critic' to draw up a chair and begin talking right over the person, saying 'this is a whole lot of nonsense this person is saying, I mean where's the evidence' or 'yeah...yeah it will never work...blah...blah'. Although it sounds comical, the inner critical voice has had me completely debilitated and anxious about people, the future and new experiences. Nothing other than the below example would do this justice!

On all fours

I was in Morocco a few years ago with a friend. We had booked to climb the Atlas Mountains. They were a striking 2,500km length, and 4,167 m high. They extended from North-Western Africa, and separated the Atlantic and Mediterranean coastline. As we started the mountain climb, the guide was leaping like a frog from one piece of the rock to the other, and my friend was mirroring his every move. That's when it happened! I looked to the right and downwards at the height from which I had come. I saw the thin netting, and all of a sudden I began holding fiercely to the rock on my left. All I could hear was the inner critic shouting 'you are going to die in the mountains, who told you to come this far? You should never have come up here?'. The more I listened, was the more I was slowly easing my way to the rock beneath my feet. I was slowly falling all the way down! Before I knew it I was on all fours in the mountain bent over like a camel. I had decided I wasn't going any further, I was going to die right there in the mountain. I had a menacing several minute movie directed by my inner critic. His main actors were Fear and Anxiety, and they were giving an Oscar winning performance. I could see and hear the multiple ways in which I would die up there. Starvation would be easiest, then death by panic attack and finally, losing strength and falling through the net. These were some of the trailers in my mind! Fear had gripped me, and I was paralysed. No one behind me could get past, and no-one returning from the opposite direction could move. I had blocked the way! I was so embarrassed and I was petrified at the same time. I wanted to climb higher but I couldn't move. The guide came back like my personal Superman lifting me from the rubble, I mean the rock, and grabbed me off the floor. He carried me over that narrow part of the mountain by force. I was so relieved and grateful, because I honestly planned on dying there.

I have never experienced the harrowing dark voice of defeat, as I did that day when I took to the mountains of the new. That experience taught me a valuable lesson:

> *'The inner critic can create an experience of grandeur, that is completely opposite to what the moment presents. You must learn to distinguish the difference between the two'.*

Half of the warfare in my mind was not about the experience beyond me, but within.

You may not be stuck in a literal mountain, but you may face a moment of ruptured faith like me, somewhere in your life's journey. The positive optimism, trust and confidence in a greater future, may be breaking. Your fears may be brewing, and the enormity of the task ahead may be great. It may feel like a mountain of struggle towards your calling, as 'the critic' in you chips away. But don't be bullied like I was. Don't become a victim of a stubborn old mind-set and voice, that wants to tame your destiny to the old, fight back. I did!

After that embarrassing incident, I was determined not to be defeated. I travelled to Montenegro, 3 years after, and I chose the highest mountain Lovcen, which was 1,749m high. The temperature was minus degrees, but I was determined to take the climb! Every time I heard the words of defeat, I stopped and spoke to myself, as crazy as I looked to everyone around. 'You aren't going to die Sharlette, breathe!'. It wasn't anything deep and spiritual, I just had to encourage myself, to keep on going one step at a time. As I approached the top of the mountain, the view was mind-blowing. As I watched clouds slothfully crawling by the clear blue skies, and looked across of several peaked mountains, I stood in awe! It was a new vision, a whole new world up there and incredibly still. I marvelled at the beauty of Gods magnificent architecture, as the mountains framed the country.

It was more than a mountain climb, it was strength of mind, heart and spirit. It was grit, determination and a time to confront my own fears!

At times you have to physically open your mouth and 'speak the power of life' (Pro 18:21), in order to counteract the negative words, you are hearing. Encourage yourself in Gods truth. Don't lay down and let the enemy walk all over you. God has given you His word, that's a weapon you get to use, so use it!

Begin by *'casting down everything that seeks to exalt itself above the knowledge of God, and take captive every thought'* (2 Cor 10:4-5). To do this, you must learn to be alert and sober minded, concerning the times when the inner voice comes into play! At times you will have to write down what is being said, and what moments lead to those feelings of self-doubt, fear, frustrations and nervousness. Are there patterns? Oftentimes, you will find that there are, because the mind likes rhythms and cycles. Recognising them, is the first step in disrupting them.

I have found that after a long day of flustering work and a demanding week, that I am always more susceptible to critical conversations. I am also more vulnerable when I am under immense pressure and my emotions are already high.

By taking the time to identify the moments when the inner voice is loudest, you may find that some of you are most at risk of hearing the inner critic when you are tired, not in control, under the influence of drugs and alcohol, or under immense stress. For some, it may be when you have not prepared for a meeting or event, or when you are on your own, isolated. Take the time to be spiritually self-aware! Developing this as a practice, may feel tiresome initially, but you've got to pull through.

Lesson two: The inner critic will throw your sacrifices at you

'Our inside critic has intimate knowledge of us and can zero in our weakest spots'
(Susan Ariel Rainbow Kennedy)

I encountered a critical taunting that was quite unusual, not so long ago.

I have nestled in the love, comfort and support, of my family over the years. They have always embraced me with encouragement, hugs, laughter and incredible support. No matter what season of life I have faced they have always been there. I honestly don't know where I would be without them! Our bond is stronger now that it has ever been, to the glory of God.

As I pursued God, and focused my time and dedication in developing community projects for my women's ministry, there was a shift in the way that the inner critic was attacking me. Instead of running through the front door with the grenades, he was sneaking through the back door with a silencer. That's when I learnt that inner critic will use your sacrifices against you.

I remember sitting with my family on a Sunday. We had all eaten, and were sharing stories whilst watching my dad's list of saved videos. He likes to store them up in the week for our arrival. As I looked around the room, I began to feel deeply inadequate that I didn't have a home filled with my own family, I couldn't do husband and wife trips to exotic locations, I had no-one to hug during family movie time and I mean the special, warm face to face hugs. There was no spouse waiting for me after a hard long day, no date nights, and it nearly brought me to tears by the time I arrived home. That night, I chose to resist entertaining the feeling, instead I reaffirmed audibly that I loved my family. I said it out loud although no-one was there. I wanted the inner critic to hear, although I am sure whispering would've had the same impact. Truth be told, I was cut, but I wasn't about to bleed out without retaliating in prayer. Now there are times when I'm cute with prayers and there are times when I have to get up and under a thing, and it was the latter.

> *Whenever you are wounded in your spirit, you may cry through the night, but at some point you have to get back up swinging!*

It was an unusual strategy of affliction, because the critical voice was not attacking me based on the new areas I was venturing into with my work and projects, but he was taking me from the side, using my own desires against me. The things I sacrificed and waited for, were being used to wound my faith and confidence. I was feeling insecure and overwhelmed, but there was nothing that the 'inner critic' was saying, that was a lie. It was true that I desired those things, but I was made to feel inwardly broken, as the voice counselled me with statements, such as: 'you've not received any gain in your desires since the last time you took a step of faith, why would you sacrifice more?', 'look around you, your sacrifice is in vain?'

This experience taught me a key lesson. When the inner critic attacks you in this fashion, it is to wound you in your emotion and draw you out into your soulish desires. The aim is to magnify your losses and sacrifices, even your worst fears, so that it's almost impossible for you to progress. The strategy seeks to depreciate your value, and make you feel like you're at a deficit because you don't have particular things. For you it could be a spouse, a car, a house or a job role. It may be the fame, the children or the wealth. What you have to do is remind yourself that the sacrifice is worth it and not in vain. You are not trying to lose the desire for 'good things'. There's nothing wrong with wanting those things, but you have a mature understanding that causes you to *'seek first the kingdom of God, and His righteousness; and all these things shall be added unto you'* (Matt 6:33).

Don't respond to the inner critic from a place of impatience, where you start getting frustrated trying to make life work harder or faster than it is. Instead, remain sober and conscious that you are playing your part according to His will, and everything that you need you will have at the right time.

Defeating the inner critic with courage

Unshackling yourself from your own limiting beliefs and the inner critical voice, takes courage.

Courage is *'the ability to do something that frightens you'*.

Despite the negative taunts within you have to keep going!

Scripture mentions courage, over 114 times in various translations, because it's one of the greatest assets in your arsenal. And as such, much of the criticism you will receive in life, seeks to destroy your courage, because you can't take risk and steps of faith without it. It takes courage to love again after you've been broken, to see yourself as someone of value when you've been told you're nothing. It takes courage to trust a path you don't always understand. It takes courage to start a business, begin a ministry, start a relationship, sign a deal, make an investment or end it. It takes courage to apply for a new role you may not be qualified or experienced in. It takes courage to learn about a new sector or group of people, and run towards them. It takes courage to occupy your spheres, and not compromise your values or vision.

In my experience, there have been more people championing me on as I've written this book, as I've flowed in my prophetic gift, as I've established my ministry, as I've created new partnerships, and enjoyed new connections. I've seen more open doors and opportunities than I could've imagined, to share, serve and learn from others. But it's not just me.

Famous author Brene Brown, details in her book on 'How the courage to be vulnerable transforms the way we live, love, parent and lead', that study after study shows the majority of people are actually rooting for you to do well in life. A large number of people in this time of your life actually want to see you thrive, and they will admire the courageous steps you are choosing to take. So in essence, some of the decisions you are fighting with, that are leading to greater opportunity to serve and transform others, would largely be embraced by a majority.

What have you been holding back on that you need to do? What courageous steps do you need to take?

It may feel uncomfortable, it may make you feel vulnerable or exposed, but trust Gods leading.

> *The very decisions you need to make in this season, the conversation and activities, could actually be the source of your greatest strength and motivation. Don't let the inner critic restrain you!*

Lesson three: Destroying through the language of love

> *New people will always be attracted to you as long as you are living in the light of your callings. However, being attracted to you doesn't mean they authentically like you!*

Be careful of new people who say they love you, but don't really know you. Even Jesus was betrayed by a disciple named Judas' betraying kiss (Matt 26:48)

Vain affections for the courageous and admirable, are winning the way in the 21st century in a culture where 'babe I love you', 'I just love you', 'I love everything about you', has become the in thing to say, with no real substance behind it. Half of these people don't even know you!

Affirmations are the in thing! However, you must be careful that you do not allow your life to be built on this as a foundation. Instead, be mindful of who invites themselves into your life through stroking your ego, and appeasing your weaknesses. Inwardly, some people are deeply critical and inquisitive, of your new found strength.

One afternoon, I was led to look at the scripture in Judges about Samson. It was incredibly telling! Delilah was a woman from the bible whose beauty and prowess seduced a strong, gifted, courageous and anointed man, handpicked by God. His name was Samson (Judges 16:7-22). Her strategy was not to destroy him through taunts, snares and abusive words, but through her cunning 'love and admiration' of his gifts, strength and talents. As she did Samson confided in her sharing his deepest secrets and his strengths. As he slept, Delilah cut his hair, which was an outward reflection of his inner strength. This exposed his weakness. When Samson awoke, his hair and strength was gone.

As I reflected on the story, I could see the lesson clearly. It reminded me of the quote by John Wooden:

> *'You can't let praise or criticism get to you.*
> *It's a weakness to get caught up in either*
> *one'.*

In life, you must be mindful of those who use their love and praise for you, to control, destroy, belittle or manipulate you. Delilah may have used cunning words, but so will others.

If the essential belief around who you are, is coming from the people beyond you, it is dangerous. The key anchor to the Spirit, should be the words of God.

Some people are internally critical of what you have, and are just drawing close through kind words to exploit who you are. You must be careful and discerning about who you trust. Don't rely on people to prop you up, no matter how close or loyal they are to you. You may enjoy encouragement here and there, but when you find people continuously digging for your weaknesses, forcing themselves into your space, you need to be watchful.

As I have emerged, I have prayerfully asked for wisdom to discern who is genuinely for me or not. I love and embrace all people, but I'm also very discerning. God has really taught me to pray about who surrounds me at all times, because it helps you to avoid unnecessary pain. I've seen God's words reveal the thoughts and intents of the heart. (Hebrews 4:12) And I've even created a distance between myself and some people, based on the wisdom of the Spirit.

May you see in this season, all those masquerading in the dark. It may be a Cain who is angry and seeks your life, it could be a Judas, a close friend whose been with you for years, but turns their back. It may be a Saul, who only loves you as long as your beneath them or serving their interests, or it could be a Peninnah who uses social media, messages, and sly remarks to taunt you. Whatever and whoever it is, may you see them clearly.

Lesson four: Disappointing others

'I'm not in this world to live up to your expectations and you're not in this world to live up to mine'

– Bruce Lee

I remember making a decision to leave a position in an organisation, and it meant moving on from a good team. On my last day, I remember another team leader approaching me and saying: 'Whatever you do please don't change'. I knew at the heart, there was something unique and beautiful, that they didn't want me to lose, and those good virtues I would do well to preserve. Although, I was conscious of her good intentions, I was also aware that at every stage of spiritual and personal growth, there are qualities, character traits and values, that will take on greater significance throughout life. Each calling will require an emergence, a new way of thinking and a need for change.

Her comments reminded me of how you can buy into the illusive idea, that you are able to stay constantly who you are today when we are all subject to change! But it could be argued that she was aware of the change, and that her assertion was that the Sharlette up ahead in life had the potential to be less than, whatever her idea of me was in the moment. Whatever the case, you must grasp this whole truth:

> *'There is a deeper rebirth and emergence that happens, when you die to the fantasies that others hold about you'*

You will change, whether intentionally or through the process of time. Your character, values, ideas, thoughts and direction, are going through swift and subtle changes throughout life. Sure, it's easier to think that people will be the same yesterday today and forevermore, that they will behave in a way that pleases you, and fulfil your expectations of who they should be, but it's unrealistic.

Nobody is created to fit into a neatly compressed box, so don't be confined to people's limited plans for your life. You must learn to stop all the worrying about what people will think or what they will say and do, as you emerge. People will talk either way. If you live how they want you to, someone will criticise you, if you don't live the way they want you to, someone will criticise you. It doesn't matter how you choose to live your life, someone will find a reason to project their insecurities and their negative thoughts and feelings onto you.

> *Some people will be upset, because you are not the person they want you to be! You have to learn to be okay with that.*

Lesson five: Loyalty Betrayal

Loyalty is concerned with support and allegiance. Loyalty forms part of the constructs for long lasting and trusting relationships. It speaks of commitment and an unwavering in your connection with a said person or organisation. It's sought after and prized, but what happens when your calling with God means that your time, energy, commitments and activities with people or places has to change?

In order to honour your loyalty to the calling on your life, some of you will have to make decisions you've avoided for years. It may mean leaving a relationship, role, position, organisation or country. That, to me, is a symbol of a higher level of service and calling, that may require risks that others call betrayal.

The reality is, that some departures are interpreted as deep betrayals by those on the receiving end. Sometimes it's the way people leave, that draws great criticism. There's no notice, no connection with co-workers, no completion of tasks, there's no-one in the reigns you've trained up, and a lot of negative press you left on the way out! That's a poor way to leave. Gratitude manners and professionalism always go a long way! Now you may say, they treated me bad, they hung me out to dry, I endured so much pain and hurt. I get that, but my question is, did you learn lessons? Did you grow from it? If so, then they played their part in your learning, and your teachers should be graced with some level of respect as you depart.

You may have to up and go based on Gods directive, but leave well and in order. Have the necessary uncomfortable conversations, be willing to hear genuine shock and disappointment at your departure, or even excitement. But don't become engulfed in the concerned that everyone doesn't understand your choices, why should they? They haven't seen the dreams you've seen or the read the words that you have, so be gracious towards them and pray for their understanding.

Generally, the people you are loyal to, imagine that you would help to serve their dreams and ambitions, protecting your relationship with integrity and commitment. When this is broken, individuals can often feel deeply hurt and disappointed. They may become great critics of everything you are seeking to embark on. Or they can handle you differently with love and grace. The latter has been my experience.

After 20 years at my prior Church, it was incredibly hard to leave, but I knew that God was calling me away. He whispered it through dreams and showed me through scripture. It was a tough decision because I consider myself to be a very loyal person, and when God puts me somewhere I don't move unless He says. I served as a Reverend as part of the Core Ministerial Team, overseeing several ministry leaders across the church. I had lectured as part of the theological institution and even served several years before in the youth department. I had long term relationships with the congregation, deep relationships with colleagues, years of serving, and a whole community of Young Adults that I lead. I was incredibly nervous to share my departure with my Bishop, but he is a loving, wise and understanding man whose integrity speaks volumes. Throughout our conversations my Bishop handled me with grace and kindness. He prayed throughout my transition and even blessed me with sentiments of reflection from my time in the church. The send-off was overwhelming, and there was such peace and love, amidst the tears and sorrow in my heart. I am eternally grateful for the lessons I learnt. But, I have often wondered, why it is that others experience such adversity, from those who hear of their departure. Why do people begin to distance themselves and even treat that person as an outsider?

Whether it is you leaving, or you're having to say goodbye to someone-else who is, it's time to 'let all bitterness, wrath, anger, clamour and evil speaking' go. (Eph 4:31-32) To let your own ego die for the greater good! For the gospel!

'We all have a role to play, the significance of that role is not restricted to any place or any one system'.

Kathryn Kuhlman

At times, you may be harshly criticised for a choice, that God gave every sign in Heaven, that you should make. Some of the worst things may be said about you after you have left, that you never heard uttered whilst you were there. It can be the hardest thing to push through, but you can't stop the criticism. You can't stop the genuine loss and grief, that others may feel at your departure. You can't dictate how they should behave and when. I'm not saying this is easy, even I have disappointed people's expectations of me to lead in particular organisations at work, to take on opportunities, to stay in some relationships, or remain in good roles. But in time you will learn to:

*'let go of who people thought you would be
for them, and to embrace who God created
you to be for Him'.*

The disciples who followed Jesus, thought He would remain loyal to them to the end, being present in the earth. And yet, it was destined that Jesus would die on the cross and be separated from them, in order to fulfil His purpose (John 18, Matt 27). In return, the disciples were given a new opportunity, to live without Jesus physically present. They found new strength as they learnt to depend on the Holy Spirit who would lead them as they transformed the world (Acts 2).

*'Separation is often Gods way of inviting
new collaborations for a greater goal and
greater good'*

Maybe your reliance on particular people or structures, have actually become debilitating instead of promoting independence and growth? Have some of you been loyal to organisations and roles, not because they are places that provide stimulation, growth or development, but because you do not want to betray friends, managers, spouses, leaders and others expectations of you? Are you wrestling with the feeling that you are letting people down!

Well you've come this far, and my advice to you is to run towards the people and places you are called to. Stop holding back from God's leading because of your own sense of loyalty to a place, position or previous calling? You've got to have the courage to go where He leads you and to stick to the plan. Remaining in opposition to the pathway God has will only frustrate your purpose.

Lesson six: Growth

In this last lesson, I want to encourage you that some criticism is God's way of showing you that things need to change. It's because of His love for you that He corrects you. (Prov 3:12)

You may have shunned criticism in times past, seeing it as a personal attack, because of your own uncertainties. Maybe the words of others were fuel to an already engulfing fire of self-criticism. But gaining feedback, ought not to be seen as bad. Sometimes God is providing you with necessary wisdom and insight into an area of your life, and you keep dismissing it.

> 'You're calling them haters, but Gods calling it truth'

Before disregarding every comment that you don't like, pray and ask God to reveal what is true from what is false. It's far too easy to refute a negative word, because it doesn't make you feel good.

Even in my experience, the inner critic has the power to thrust the courage out of you, causing you to take the climb to higher heights in spiritual and physical growth. This journey is all about growth, which requires new information, and often times that arrives through the clashing and fusing, of different perspectives.

I've had many things said about me over the years. I'm strong, I'm too feminine, I'm too slim, I'm too sensitive, I'm too loud and too radical. I'm too soft, I'm too quiet, I've got no respect; I've got lots of respect. I care too much; I don't care enough. I'm too giving, I don't give enough. I'm too strange and I'm unconventional! The balance is constantly tilting. At the time they were said, some were hurtful, but some were true.

Critics

In the early years of my faith walk, criticism from the church really crippled my confidence, I would crumble and withdraw, but as I've grown over the years, I've learnt to handle criticism with grace. To shake off the intrusive comments, and to pray concerning the words I feel may have some semblance in my life.

As with all things in life, the key is to be honest with yourself in the journey. It doesn't hurt to change if it's in the areas you 'need' to. As you emerge there ought to be a maturity and deep inner reflection, that allows you to be more self-aware, and to acknowledge the areas where you are falling short.

CHAPTER ELEVEN

Emerge-n-cy

We've got to go

'Knocking, knocking –what still there?
Waiting, waiting grand and fair;
Yes, the pierced hand still knocketh,
And beneath the crowned hair
Beam the patient eyes, so tender,
Of the Saviour, waiting there'.

-Harriet Beecher Stowe, 1876

AS YOU emerge, you must see this as the call to step forward, to come up higher. As Harriet Beecher Stowe, the abolitionist reminds us in the poem, God is waiting for each of you to respond.

Are you committed to obeying the voice of God wherever He leads in the journey of life? Because there's safety and refuge wherever He takes you.

At times you may want to argue and bargain with God over what He is asking from you, instead of submitting and answering yes through obeying His voice. But, I can candidly say that 'yes' was the best answer I gave God.

Although I had to unlearn and let go of a lot of what I thought I knew about myself, I have learnt incredible lessons that have reframed my whole perspective of life. I didn't know then what I know now, but the knocking in my life was God awakening me to more. It was God getting my attention. He was showing me where the disconnect and resistances had arisen in my life. But I had to learn to be flexible again and to listen.

My routine now embraces rest and I have time for greater balance.

As I submitted to the process of transformation, I have regained my confidence and trust in Gods eternal plan. I am not throwing myself here, there and everywhere, but I am treading my path. With it came a greater discernment than I ever imagined, and an ease to hearing God, whether He's speaking about me or about others.

God has transformed my outlook on life as I am more intentional about the gospel than I have ever been. I've learnt, and I still am, to stand up in God for myself, without all the scaffolds of people.

I have been progressing with my charity to support women and those who are sex trafficking victims, and I am finding so much meaning and value through the work. If you had told me I would be doing any of these things before, I would've laughed, but I let go of my own self-image to take on the roles that was calling me into.

I'm less stressed, and I've found joy again in reaching and transforming the world. I've got everything I need through Christ Jesus, but I am learning daily, how to let the spirit flow freely through me.

My yes, was to constantly emerge with the God of Heaven on my side, championing the gospel for humanity. And I am more determined than ever, to teach the next generation how to live sensitive to Gods voice and leading, as they navigate through life.

Of course from this point forward you have to make some decisions, but I pray that you listen to the voice of the Spirit and not the voice of fear.

All God asks is that you '*draw close to Him and He promises to draw close to you*' (James 4:8).

It's the beautiful dance of life, the embracing of two hands with your feet moving in time - flowing to the beat of an Eternal rhythm. How beautiful is that? I guess the challenge is that often times the grasping of God's hands and sensitivity to His leading, happens with joy as we enter into seasons of flourishing and joy, and at other times it happens in the midst of sufferings and hardships. Either way the lord of the dance promises that:

> '*whether you turn to the right or to the left, your ears will hear a voice behind you, saying 'This is the way; walk in it'* (Isaiah 30:21)

There is beauty is this life and its Gods desire that you are open to discovering it again. So trust the inner leading of the Spirit and be open to it, no matter where the dance takes you.

The new winding roads and the upward mountains of discovery learning are awaiting your tender feet. As you continue to open the door to those you are called to reach, may greater room be made in your spiritual houses to receive them.

As the boundaries of your understanding continue to be broadened, you can see the responsibility that each of you have to transform the world around you and to see souls saved. However, you must remember that the battle of the earth and the human soul is not yours, it is the Lords (2 Chro. 2:15), you are just His hands and feet. Remember that, and you can stay postured in that humility, as God uses you to bring wondrous transformation in the earth. This is not business as usual, no it's an intentional commitment towards your callings, because your service is needed more now than ever.

Should you step into this season open to learning and unlearning again, He will open doors to new rooms of revelation, and lead you to see the spiritual realm more real than ever before. However, there are many lessons that can't be articulated through the pages of a book; God has to teach you. So remain open.

As you continue throughout life's journey emerging, I wanted to leave this prayer with you.

Emerge, and let your enemies be scattered

God, you are sovereign and we come before you humbly, listening and waiting.

We thank you for choosing to love us - those of us who know you and those who deny you ever existed. You love each person the same and unconditionally. And with all our busyness in life, it's still a wonder that we are even on your mind.

We are sorry that we became so lost in the world, in the business and activities, that we could no longer hear the quiet knocking in our hearts. We are sorry for the times we have wandered off the path to do things our own way, and stubbornly kept on doing it, even though the tug in our spirit was telling us to stop. But you have our attention now, and we know you have been fighting for it.

Let our deafened ears be open, so that we hear with sensitivity each sound of the spirit, from the whispers to the shouts.

As we begin to discern your manifested presence in our lives we won't be afraid of the new and the unknown because you are in it. So we ask that you let the unknown become known as we travel through life.

Awaken us to the supernatural power of the Holy Spirit, visiting us through dreams, unusual encounters and visions.

The winds of change are here and you are beckoning us forward, so let them blow, let them pass over the earth and draw back the tide even as you did with Noah. And as we move towards you in deeper prayer and learning, may you draw nigh to us with your Eternal light, because you are light. (John 1:5). We ask you to expose and illuminate the darkness in our lives. Reveal the activities, worries and behaviours, that have caused us to lose the fragile beauty of peace, and let us reacquaint with it again.

Sweet rest, sweet times of stillness and reflection are invited in. We open the door to that new fragrance in our lives, of deep inner peace and rest. May it saturate our homes, our families and our lives, as we realign and reprioritise our daily activities.

As you did in Genesis 1:3, we ask you speak again and show us greater revelation, so that we can discover the path ahead of us - our callings. We commit to more intentional time as we connect with your word through daily worship and prayer, so teach us how to trust your promises as you unveil your plans.

Remove the briars, weeds and fences that we have erected, to keep ourselves far away from the pain and sufferings of the world, and open our ears to hear it again, with compassion. As we do we will prayerfully stand in the gap for those we are too far to physically touch.

We lean into the moving tides of the Spirit as you lead us, and we ask that you teach us how to listen again. We want to run and walk to a new rhythm, and live to a new beat – completely in sync with you.

Focus is what we need lord, so I pray that the distractions beyond us and the distractions within, would come to a hush as we spend time away from the noise. We refuse to be targeted in our minds and backed up against a wall like a victim enslaved to activity. Instead we cry out for our generation of men and women, sons and daughters. Let there be an emerging!

Let the blind eyes be open to perceive the world the way that you do. Help us to be conscious and aware, as we look through a new spiritual lens. Because the crisis of the human spirit, is no longer something we will remain numb to, so soften our hearts and renew our minds, concerning our fellow man.

For those who are broken in spirit, in body and in heart, let them receive divine and supernatural healing even as they close the last page of this book. And let that be an ensign of a new beginning, a new wholeness and deeper walk.

We pray that cancers, leukaemia, issues of the blood, wombs that have been closed, mental health diagnosis, and paralysis be healed. Even the old wounds that have leaked into the passages of our lives, destroyed our relationships and distorted personalities, be permanently closed as we cry out to you.

We in this generation are responding to the call, and this isn't the season to compromise or hold back, but to keep advancing in the spirit. However, we are not asking you for the ordinary but the power of the extraordinary God. Even as you empowered the apostles in the upper room for service in Acts 2, we ask you to show us a new room, a new land and a new spiritual Plainfield.

Let us enjoy greater freedom, greater rest and fulfilment.

This time we are choosing to live sold out, and more flexible to the leading of the Spirit. We just ask that you help us in moments of weakness to say yes to it all.

'We will fear no evil because you are with us' (Psalms 23:4)

This is our radical commitment to share the gospel with those around us, with the short time we have on this earth. To play our part using our flint and our diamonds.

We recognise the value of the strangers in the coffee shops, on the streets that we pass, in the supermarkets, and we are committed to reaching those we need to.

We ask for the divine connections, provisions and opportunities to change the world – to inspire and touch another life. We want to feel the pull greater than before, towards those that we need to speak to, encourage, pray for and help.

We are leaving the old and calling forth into the new. So as we break from the comforts and safe spaces, to take the risk and reach others, we do it with new boldness. As we run towards the world with open arms, we ask for a greater spiritual strength to contend with the darkness of this age. Give us the strength to stand amidst the economic, political and social shifts that will come. As you said in your word, *'when the enemy comes in like a flood, the Spirit of the Lord shall lift up a standard against him'* (Isa 59:19) and we stand on that word.

Though we may become wearied, we pray that you lift up our hands and raise our arms in surrender to your plan. At times the light may feel like a flickering torch, but we will still keep listening and moving in the direction you lead.

Let the inner conviction of salvation be the anchor, when the storms of life are raging. And when the answers are not arriving as quick as we would like, help us to be patient in prayer with understanding, this way we can free ourselves from unnecessary sufferings.

When the afflictions of the dark seasons want to silence us, we will open our mouth and stand on our feet using the transformative power on the inside of us. *'For we do not wrestle against flesh and blood, but against principalities, powers and rulers of darkness'* (Eph 6:12) So we declare that the enemy of our soul is under our feet, and we won't let Him steal, kill and destroy our divine destiny.

Help us to grow and learn from criticism, and not to retreat and isolate ourselves. Draw those who have been concealed for years by the fears and opinions of other people, and let them dare to be more. Our inner critical voice will not cause us to stumble as we take the climb to higher heights in you.

The world can't hold us back, because we are coming forth!

Though there will be a scattering as a result of shifts and changes in the world beyond, and mixed opinions and views, we pray that *'the word will be a lamp to our feet and a light to our pathway'* (Psa 119:105). Let this not destroy our faith, but strengthen it.

As we connect to the Eternal movement, we follow you forward into our new day, to 'go forth and multiply'.

We choose to emerge - because we believe there's more!

Amen

CHAPTER TWELVE

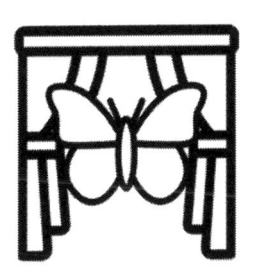

Emerge

THIS BOOK is not just challenging you to change or evolve, which refers to a gradual development and change over time, as everything in the world evolves sometimes for good and sometimes for bad. But you have been given an incredible gift to emerge. That means that with each change in your life and each new journey, you are listening to the Holy Spirit. You are becoming more flexible and intentional about *'moving away from what concealed and hid you'*. Each step brings a greater unveiling and revelation of you are.

Greater distance is created from the old, as you soar further and further away from your own fears and anxieties, challenging yourself to take the climb higher and higher, with greater trust in God. This level of growth allows you to *'become visible'* to new people, in new spheres and new places. That journey never stops, as you reach people with compassion and love.

It's time for you to recognise that like the caterpillar, you have everything you need to soar, to transform, and to live out a higher level of service than you currently are. But, until you can commit to intentional growth and development in the journeys of life, you will remain in the cocoon with all the potential stored on the inside, to break free and emerge.

You have to make the investment of time to seek your own pathway with the Holy Spirit as your guide, and if you do, you will find it. That direction and course may not arise from the signposts beyond you that indicate you must go this way or that way, or make that choice or decision. But instead, you will learn to recognise the signposts within, the deep discernment, the knocking, the gentle leading and quiet whispers of the Spirit.

Learn to grow in life with an openness to flexibility and change, because that for most, will be and has been, the greatest challenge. Should you learn to be open throughout life, flexible to the winds of change, then you too can learn to be free from your own limitations. You can learn to appreciate the lessons and developmental stages that have brought you so far, the environments, people, thoughts, roles, positions and emotions. You can cast off the illusive sense of 'arrival', because you are fully conscious that there is far more to be discovered about God, yourself and life.

No-ones coming to announce to you that it's time to break free, if you are not ready to break free for yourself. You must recognise, change is here, it's waiting for you to see that you were called for more.

It's time to leave the cocoon and unwrap your beautiful wings, taking flight as you pursue life's callings, ascending to heights of service and fulfilment that you never imagined. That is the destruction of the old and the beginning of the new unknown. This is the life of risk, faith and even the unexplainable, should you commit to it.

As I part ways for now, the rest of the journey awaits.

> *Look to the future with great expectation, because God will do greater things in this generation. Now let us end with this declaration:*

When I live out my commitment to emerge, I can be free from the inner tensions that arise when I ignore, dismiss and frustrate Gods purpose for me.

I can be emancipated from the oppression of old ways of thinking, through renewal in God's word. No longer living in palaces of past pains, fears and anxieties.

I can, through biblical teachings and a connection to the Holy Spirit, learn to see God, my world and myself anew, through discovery learning.

I can invite into each new morning through prayer, God's guidance, leading, rest and daily healing into my life.

I can surrender in peace, my deep internal struggles for control, and my plans, to the Eternal plan and movement of God.

I can perceive the new and unknown, entering into new spheres and frontiers, in the spiritual world and the natural world; transforming people in industry, community, nations, sectors and groups.

I can begin to see the world with a new gaze unfazed by critics

And finally, I can find my place in the world, liberated and liberating others, through the gospel of Jesus Christ.

- Selah

The 12 phases of Emerging

Chapter	Symbol	Principle
1 Knocking	🚪	Be open
2 Fast and focus	👁	Lower the noise
3 Naked	🌳	Let healing flow
4 Core	🧠	Humility opens the door for more
5 Unexpected change	🪧	Change carves a new path
6 The lost virtue	🕐	Patience is your friend
7 The flint, the diamonds and the compass	💎🧭	Talents, gifts and compassion for the win
8 Strangers	👥	New people are valuable
9 Extraction	🧰	Serving goes two ways
10 Critics	🎙	Take the climb
11 Emerg-en-cy	🌅	The world is calling
12 Emerge	🚪	Come forth

Acknowledgements

I thank God for His inspiration and revelation. I am also grateful for life's experience and the dream I had back in 2016 of writing this book.

I am truly thankful for my mother, father, sister and brothers, who have always championed the need for me to step out and do more; Lynnette Dias, (Fei), Cherelle Reid and Rose Reid, thanks for inspiring me with constant probes about when the book will be complete. You have all been valuable beyond words in this journey.

Thanks to Jacqui Ewers for your long conversations and wise advice throughout my writing journey.

Thanks to my spiritual scaffolds, Bishop Delroy Powell, Bishop John Francis, Bishop Noel Mclean, Min. Annemarie and Eld. Jacqui H, you have prayerfully and wisely strengthened my journey.

I am indebted to the Emerge Worldwide team: Daniel, Storm, Ruth, Keeley, Kesha and Shakura, for the giving of your time. You've given your hearts, energy and input in building a vision based on liberating the masses, as they pursue a higher calling.

Thanks to my family for loving and supporting me throughout my life.

Thanks to all the children I get to teach, and who have taught me incredible lessons throughout life's journey. It's an honour to play a part in the future of our world.

Finally, a huge thankyou to everyone who has bought this book. Each of you have played a role in supporting me as I emerge, and I look forward to meeting you some day, in this life or the next!

We all serve at the Kings pleasure - Emerge

Notes

CHAPTER 1
1. Environmental-noise-guidelines-for-the-european-region 2018, accessed July 2020, https://www.euro.who.int/en/health-topics/environment-and-health/noise/publications/2018/
2. Ron Chepesiuk, 'Decibel hell: the effects of living in a noisy world'. Journal of the Environ Health Perspect. 2005 Jan; 113(1): A34–A41.
3. Einstein, Albert, Ideas and Opinions, (Crown Publishers, Inc., New York 1954). A 1995 edition

CHAPTER 2
1. Human Multitasking, accessed 11th July 2019 https://en.wikipedia.org/wiki/Human_multitasking
2. Caroline Beaton, How Multitasking is changing our brains, accessed June 2019 https://www.forbes.com/sites/carolinebeaton/2017/01/27/the-millennial-workforce-how-multitasking-is-changing-our-brains/?sh=578f30833605
3. Stress and the Mind, accessed 11th June 2019 https://www.mind.org.uk/
4. Matthew J. Edlund M.D, 'The Power of Rest', accessed 19th January 2020, https://www.psychologytoday.com/gb/blog/the-power-rest/201110/why-we-dont-get-rest
5. https://dictionary.cambridge.org/

CHAPTER 3.
1. Hillary Hoffower and Allana Akhtar, 'Lonely, burned out, and depressed: The state of millennials' mental health in 2020' Pew Research Centre, accessed on the 3rd March 2020 https://www.businessinsider.com/millennials-mental-health-burnout-lonely-depressed-money-stress?r=US&IR=T
2. Blue Cross Blue Shields Report (2019), accessed 25th February 2019 https://www.bcbs.com/sites/default/files/file-attachments/health-of-america-report/HOA-Moodys-Millennial-10-30.pdf
Zoë Chance, Michael I. Norton, Francesca Gino, and Dan Ariely, 'Temporal view of the costs and benefits of self-deception', PNAS September 13, 2011 108 (Supplement 3) 15655-15659; first published March 7, 2011; https://doi.org/10.1073/pnas.1010658108
Edited by Donald W. Pfaff, The Rockefeller University, New York, NY, and approved January 28, 2011

3. Wellbeing of Mind accessed 11th October 2019 https://www.mind.org.uk/
4. Creating a positive self-image BeReal, accessed 12th August 2020 https://www.berealcampaign.co.uk/
5. Dove Self Esteem Project, accessed April 2019 https://www.dove.com/uk/dove-self-esteem-project.html
6. BBC Report, Skin is not for likes (2020), accessed October 2020 https://youtu.be/_9D2S07wxd0

CHAPTER 4
1. OWN Oprah Winfrey interview with Daniel Day Lewis (2012) accessed on the 14th January 2018 https://youtu.be/5g9v8y5FvS0
2. OWN Oprah Winfrey interview with Nelson Mandela (2013), accessed 2nd May 2018 https://youtu.be/t1hZ-z6aoHs
3. Pride and a controlling nature (2007) Mind Renewal Self-Help pdf http://mindrenewal.us/page6.html
4. Smith, R. H. (2000). Assimilative and contrastive emotional reactions to upward and downward social comparisons. In J. Suls & L. Wheeler (Eds.), The Plenum series in social/clinical psychology. Handbook of social comparison: Theory and research (p. 173–200). Kluwer Academic Publishers. Accessed 31st September 2019 https://doi.org/10.1007/978-1-4615-4237-7_10
5. Roseman, I. J., Antoniou, A. A., & Jose, P. E. (1996). Appraisal determinants of emotions: Constructing a more accurate and comprehensive theory. Cognition and Emotion, 10, 241–27
6. Micheal Josephus, 'Quotations on Human Character' accessed 13th July 2019 https://whatwillmatter.com/2013/10/quotations-character-reputation-character-education-best-quotes-ever/

CHAPTER 5
1. Arnold Bennett - The Great Adventure: "Any change, even a change for the better is always accompanied by drawbacks and discomforts." Paperback – 28 Feb. 2014
by Arnold Bennett (Author)
2. https://www.challies.com/articles/defining-discernment/
3. https://www.barclays.co.uk/smart-investor/news-and-research/experts/robert-smith/

CHAPTER 6
1. Sarah Schnitker, 'An examination of patience and well-being', July 2012, The Journal of Positive Psychology 7(4):263-280

2. Louisa C. Michl, Katie A. McLaughlin, Kathrine Shepherd, Susan Nolen-Hoeksema 'Rumination as a Mechanism Linking Stressful Life Events to Symptoms of Depression and Anxiety: Longitudinal Evidence in Early Adolescents and Adults' Journal of Abnormal Psychology. 2013 May; 122(2): 339–352.

CHAPTER 7

1. Christina Rossetti, 'An Emerald is as green as grass', accessed 13th December 2019 https://www.poetrybyheart.org.uk/poems/an-cmerald-is-as-green-as-grass/
2. Sir Ken Robinson, 'Finding Your Element: How to Discover Your Talents and Passions and Transform Your Life', Published by Penguin books (2013)
3. 'Buried Talents: The Gifted Child in Church', February 16, 1962, accessed 5th June 2019 https://www.christianitytoday.com/ct/1962/february-16/buried-talents-gifted-child-in-church.html
4. Kevin Allocca, 'YouTube's Head of Culture and Trends, a rousing and illuminating behind-the-scenes exploration of internet video's massive impact on our world', Bloomsbury Publishing USA, 23 Jan 2018
5. Whitney Johnson, 'Why Talented People Don't Use Their Strengths', Harvard Business Review, accessed on the 2nd February 2019, https://hbr.org/2018/05/why-talented-people-dont-use-their-strengths
6. Wayne Grudem, 'Systematic Theology: An Introduction To Biblical Doctrine' Grand Rapids, Mich: Zondervan 2000
7. The Meaning of Compassion, accessed 5th October 2020 https://www.compassionuk.org/blogs/what-is-compassion/ 2018
8. Child Poverty Facts and Figures, accessed on 11th May 2020 https://cpag.org.uk/child-poverty/child-poverty-facts-and-figures 2020
9. Dennis D. Tirch, Benjamin Schoendorff, Laura R. Silberstein, 'The ACT Practitioner's Guide to the Science of Compassion Tools for Fostering Psychological Flexibility' Little, Brown New Harbinger, 2015
10. Department of Statistics for South Africa, accessed 31st March http://www.statssa.gov.za/?p=13438&gclid=CjwKCAiAzNj9BRBDEiwAPsLod6U EoccxhMppEpJRBY5vVHXG8dovw2_XWbNx8ea_JcJNy9NIn9P5UBoCXCcQAv D_BwE

CHAPTER 8

1. Joanna Moorhead, 'Why casual chats with strangers are the thing many of us miss the most', accessed 9th August 2019,

https://www.theguardian.com/society/2020/may/23/why-casual-chats-with-strangers-are-the-thing-many-of-us-miss-the-most-coronavirus

2. Malcolm Gladwell, 'Talking to Strangers: What We Should Know about the People We Don't Know', Published by Little, Brown and Company 2019

3. Ellen Kate Donnelly, 'Why you shouldn't be afraid of strangers' 2018, accessed on 7th April 2019, https://medium.com/be-unique/why-you-shouldnt-be-afraid-of-strangers-74f1f9a1b408

4. Nicholas Epley and Juliana Schroeder, BBC Report on 'The Surprising Benefits of Talking to Strangers, accessed on 3rd June 2019, https://www.bbc.co.uk/news/world-4845994

CHAPTER 9

1. John S Dunne, 'Eternal Consciousness', University of Notre Dame Press (15 May 2012)

2. Merriam Webster Dictionary, accessed 14th June 2019
https://www.merriam-webster.com/

3. Shakespeare, accessed 23rd July 2020,
https://www.brainyquote.com/quotes/william_shakespeare_166828#:~:text=William%20Shakespeare%20Quotes&text=All%20the%20world's%20a%20stage%2C%20and%20all%20the%20men%20and,his%20acts%20being%20seven%20ages.

4. Viktor Kubik, 'You are unique - And God loves that uniqueness!', accessed 36th May 2020

CHAPTER 10

1. Susan Ariel Rainbow Kennedy (SARK), 'Creative Companion: How to Free Your Creative Spirit', accessed on 23rd February 2019, https://www.goodreads.com/book/show/164862.Creative_Companion

2. Brene Brown, 'Daring Greatly: How the Courage to Be Vulnerable Transforms the Way We Live, Love, Parent, and Lead Paperback', Published by Avery, 2012

3. Bruce Lee, 'I'm not in this world to live up to your expectations and you're not in this world to live up to mine' accessed on 11th September, https://www.goodreads.com/quotes/136057-i-m-not-in-this-world-to-live-up-to-your

4. Kathryn Kuhlman, 'We all have a role to play, the significance of that role is not restricted to any place or any one system', accessed 3rd June, https://www.allchristianquotes.org/authors/156/Kathryn_Kuhlman/

Printed by Amazon Italia Logistica S.r.l.
Torrazza Piemonte (TO), Italy